You are a hunter!

Why is hunting so important to you? You return year after year with high anticipation, expectation, and excitement. How did hunting become such an integral part of who you are?

What caused you to become a hunter? Who influenced you? Has your desire to hunt increased or decreased? Is your privilege to hunt in jeopardy? What do you do to improve and guarantee a hunting future?

As you read this book, take time to recall and reflect on your own hunting experience. We must continually remind ourselves of the privilege and responsibility we have as hunters.

THE HUNTER

BY BOB NORTON, PH.D.

RIVERBEND
PUBLISHING

Copyright © 2008 by Bob Norton

Published by Riverbend Publishing, Helena, Montana.

Printed in the United States of America.

All rights reserved. No part of this book may be reproduced, stored, or transmitted in any form or by any means without the prior permission of the publisher, except for brief excerpts for reviews.

ISBN 10: 1-931832-49-8
ISBN 13: 978-1-931832-49-6

Riverbend Publishing
P.O. Box 5833
Helena, MT 59604
Toll-free 1-866-787-2363
www.riverbendpublishing.com

CONTENTS

PREFACE	Page	9
CHAPTER 1 FAMILY TRADITIONS	Page	12
CHAPTER 2 THE DEVELOPMENTAL PLATEAUS	Page	26
CHAPTER 3 THE ETHICAL HUNTER	Page	54
CHAPTER 4 VIOLATORS	Page	91
CHAPTER 5 WHY DO YOU HUNT	Page	110
CHAPTER 6 THE HUNTING PARTY	Page	122
CHAPTER 7 THE SAFE HUNT	Page	136
CHAPTER 8 INFLUENCES	Page	145
CHAPTER 9 THE RESEARCH MODEL	Page	160

ACKNOWLEDGMENTS

To Marcia Johnson-Sage, who labored to read my illegible handwriting and change it to the original typed manuscript.

To Beth Friemel-Norton, who continued to encourage me, continued to type and retype the manuscript as it went through numerous changes.

To Homer Moe and John Plenke, former Wisconsin Department of Natural Resource administrators of the hunter education program. To their District Law Enforcement Safety Specialists, Bob Hoyt, Bob Tucker, Larry Keith, Bill Engfer, Rick Wolfe, and Harland Steinhorst. Their assistance in developing the research and interpretation of data and insights into hunter behavior were invaluable.

To the late Dr. David Witmer, former Vice Chancellor in charge of special projects, University of Wisconsin, La Crosse Campus. His continual support for university funding of the research project allowed us to develop the work to a professional level.

To all of the national, state, and local organizations that contributed financial support to the research. Especially to Jim Jones, Regional Federal Aid Coordinator, U.S. Fish and Wildlife Service, for his involvement by allowing us to apply for and use Pittman Robertson funds for major financial support.

To all of the hunters and non-hunters who allowed us to talk hunting with them, at times in the woods, at times in the comfort of their homes.

To all of the trained field observers, field interviewers, and in-depth home interviewers who did their work with pride and professionalism.

To my wife Carole, who always encouraged me to be involved in the project, even as its time commitment took its toll on our family life and she was willing to keep the home fires burning.

This work is dedicated:

To my mother and dad who, during my formative years, taught me to respect myself, my family, others, and, the environment by being with me and showing me love and concern. Without respect there is no meaning to life.

To my dad who took me with him into the woods and taught me to appreciate its beauty, realize its economic value, know it as a place of refuge, respect the plants and animals that reside there, and know how to harvest the resources.

To the late Dr. Bob Jackson, who I partnered with on the hunter research project, spent hours together on brook trout streams, pursued the ruffed grouse in the north woods of Wisconsin, duck hunted in the marshes of the Mississippi River bottoms, tramped the pheasant habitat of Iowa; to my colleague, hunting partner, and friend.

PREFACE

The ten o'clock weather report said rain mixed with snow and northwest wind, ten to fifteen miles per hour. As you snuggle down under the covers, you hear the wind howling and the rain beating against the side of the house. You fall asleep knowing that tomorrow will be one of those days you live for.

Four thirty, the alarm goes off. As you lay there for a moment, a fleeting thought passes through your mind that it might be easier to just stay right where you are, but you don't and you find your feet hitting the floor. You head to the kitchen, as you have so many times before, plug in the coffee pot, turn on the burner under the old frying pan, put the bacon in, and head to wash up and put on the first layer of warm clothes. As you return to the kitchen, the smell of coffee and bacon brings the first smile to your face. The bacon is done and you break a couple of eggs into the pan, then sit down and think about the day that's ahead.

Another layer of clothes is added you pick up the gun from the corner of the kitchen, make sure you have enough ammunition, and head for the truck. As you step outside the wind bites and, during the night, the rain had changed to snow, so the ground is white. You take a deep breath and the second smile appears.

As you drive out of town, the houses are all dark and there are no cars on the street, but you know where that special place is that you're heading for, and the anticipation of the day's hunt becomes real. You leave the parked truck in the dark find the old trail that leads you to that special place, and set up for the day's hunt. As the sun comes up, it feels colder than you thought, but as the darkness fades and you see the familiar surroundings, you know you're where you want to be. You settle down in the blind or on the stand, and you become part of that hunter's world where you realize that you're no greater or no less than the environment you find yourself in. You are part of it.

You're a hunter, and you realize what a privilege it is to be in the field.

Why has hunting become such an integral part of who you are? How did you start? Why did you continue? Why do you wait with such high anticipation for each season to begin and than hate to see it end? Why do you so vividly remember the time you messed up or missed and a trophy got away, yet you have difficulty recalling the ones that didn't?

Has hunting changed you or have you changed as you continued to hunt, or is it a combination of both? Over five thousand hunters related that they progressed through developmental stages, each time incorporating the past stages into the next stage, each time having a new and deeper appreciation of hunting. What stage are you at? Will you continue to progress or be content to stay where you are? Is our right to hunt in jeopardy?

Are we doing all that we can to assure continuation of our privilege to hunt?

Each time I talked with a hunter about his/her experiences, it caused me to reflect on my own passion for hunting. I hope the same will happen to you as you read on.

One of the perks of having the opportunity to interview hunters was that it caused me to reflect on hunting moments of my own. My hope is that you're reading of the book will do the same for you. The book is not intended to be a sitdown-and-read, but instead, take your time, recall your own hunting and realize how fortunate we are to live in a country that legitimizes hunting. At the beginning of each chapter there is an opportunity to jot down a few thoughts. Compare your hunting world with the responses of five thousand other hunters who were interviewed.

If you are interested in an overview of the methodology utilized in the study, go to chapter 9, page 160.

CHAPTER 1
FAMILY TRADITIONS

Remember those first years of hunting. What was it like; what started your hunting world; who were you with; why did you continue to hunt? Jot down your thoughts.

If a person could predict one's future at birth, it would have been predicted that part of my future would include my being a hunter.

My first detailed recollection of my life-long pursuit of becoming a hunter goes back to when I was five years old. I was attending first grade and living with my mother, dad, and younger sister, Sharon. I lived my first eighteen years in Northern Wisconsin with my family, which also included my youngest sister, Nancy, who was born when I was eight. My dad's primary income was from logging, as he and my grandpa owned land where they cut pulpwood that was sold to the paper mills. Dad also owned the school bus and drove for the local school system. During the summer, he operated the township-owned grader and graded the dirt roads that ran throughout the township.

As a primarily self-sustaining family, there was a large garden during the summer for vegetables that were canned for the winter months, as well as raising chickens, hogs, and beef for meat. The meat was raised at my grandpa's place and the chicken and hogs were raised at our place. In early November, the beef and hogs were butchered as the cold winter period was beginning. We had our own icehouse and ice boxes to keep the meat for future use if the weather was too warm, and a large amount of meat was canned so it could be used throughout the following summer. The butchering and processing was started in time to be completed by the late November whitetail season. When the deer season opened, all work stopped and the hunt became the reason for living.

Behind our one room log home, there was a chicken coop, a barn for the horses and a few milk cows, and the barrels and hoist for butchering hogs. The hogs were shot, lowered in and out of the barrels of hot water, scraped to remove the hair, and then dressed and left to hang. They would hang for a couple of weeks, then Dad and Grandpa would cut them up into various roasts and steaks. Those few weeks, when the hogs were hanging, became my opportunity to begin my hunting experiences.

The hogs were magnets, drawing chickadees from miles around as they came and pecked at the meat. Whenever Dad and Grandpa were around the hanging hogs, they would chase the chickadees away, and I soon figured out that it would be okay if I also tried to keep them away.

So began my hunting world. I went into the woods, cut a skinny poplar pole that was about twelve feet long and positioned myself in a manner that would allow me to hit the chickadees as they landed on the hogs. I sat, motionless, but none would come and light. Then the problem solving had to begin. I moved further away, then they came, but my stick wouldn't reach the hogs.

I would sit in school and try to anticipate my next move, and really was not interested in the alphabet and the sounds that the different letters would make. To hunt those chickadees became my primary concern and provided purpose for my thinking. When I used the long pole, it was too heavy for me to swing, so they always got away.

I tried to make blinds where I could get closer, but they always saw me, and sometimes, to add insult to injury, they would light on the end of my pole. I never got one, but I did begin to understand what challenge meant.

Now, sixty-two years later, when I am sitting in a tree stand during the bow or firearm season, and a chickadee lights on a branch next to me I can vividly see those hogs and feel the excitement and frustration of the first hunts. And I remember the warmth and love that embodied that log house that I would retreat to as the cold and darkness would set in. Hunting has a tradition.

The whitetail hunting season dominated the hunting world of my dad, grandpa, and uncles. There was constant discussion that pertained to the whitetail: the size of the herd, how they had wintered, the fawn crop, where big bucks were being sighted, the stories of last year's hunt, stories of excitement and experience of past hunts, some stories of big bucks getting away, and some that didn't, stories of smart old bucks that would always disappear the day or two before the season began, the folklore of the whitetail. I was in constant contact with the hunters and listened to their stories and dreamed of the day when I could join their ranks. My hunting identity was forming.

Dad, Grandpa, Uncle Glen, Uncle Carl, Uncle John, Uncle Dan, Uncle Cully, each one was an individual, each one a hunter in his own right, some consistently more successful with the harvest, but each one lived the anticipation and excitement of the hunt. The whitetail provided a nucleus that drew the men together, provided a common denominator for talk, stories, laughter, and ultimately, for the opportunity to prove themselves. There was no competition between them, and they embellished in each other's success. They were my role models throughout the year; they became my heroes during the hunting season.

At completion of the first day of the hunt, they would gather at Grandpa's and Grandma's house or stop at our place and the sense of oneness of purpose and family permeated the house. All were tired, dressed in red and black wool shirts and black wool pants, all pleased with the day's hunt, checking out stories and developing strategies for the next day's hunt. The first days of the hunt were normally spent in individual hunts or father-son combinations. Dad and Grandpa always hunted together and I was fortunate to have the opportunity to have one season of going with both of them during Grandpa's last year to hunt.

By Wednesday of hunting season, plans were made for the hunting patterns to change, as Thursday, Thanksgiving Day, started the hunting party and the strategy was to gather and join forces. The traditional evening Thanksgiving meal was always at Grandma's house, where the men would meet at daybreak to begin the day's hunt. Mom and my aunts would arrive early afternoon with food and my cousins, and the celebration would begin.

Grandpa's and Grandma's log house sat upon a knoll surrounded by large pine trees and the hill slanted down to a small swamp that encircled about half the knoll. We slid, ran, wrestled, and played a game that mimicked whitetail hunting. Some of us would tie small branches to our heads to project the image of horns and we would become a whitetail. We would then go into the woods and hide, with the right to run, and when the hunters came after us, they had to poke us with their stick gun to harvest us. The person playing the part of the whitetail had more prestige than the hunter. During November, this was also the most popular game at school.

By late afternoon, we kids were tired and we began to await the return of the hunters. I can vividly remember my excitement. I was only six or seven years old, but I already knew what the hunt meant to the family and the excitement of the anticipation of the hunters returning. They were often successful and brought in a whitetail or two. Then the meal, talking and laughter, as we celebrated the hunt and Thanksgiving.

Grandma died the summer of my eighth year, and Grandpa came to live in a house dad built for him, next to our place, and the big family Thanksgiving meals changed as each family became more self-centered. The hunting pattern did not change, as Dad and Mom's place became the meeting place of the hunters. Mom would be up before daybreak, putting the coffee on, starting the bacon, warming up the fried potatoes, and then the final touch, cooking the eggs as the men gathered. By daylight they would all leave and then the long wait for darkness and their return. At eight years old, my hunting world was framed.

The future of hunting rests in the young hunters; they will become the dedicated hunters that will keep the tradition. Without them, hunting has no future. We become concerned with the anti-hunters, the movement of pay-to-hunt that has become a booming business, the elimination of the "slob" hunters who give fellow hunters a poor image, and hunting techniques that lower the quality of a hunt, but none of these legitimate concerns will make any difference if young boys and girls do not enter the fraternity and become part of the hunting tradition.

Every state has a hunter education program for first time hunters. Bob Jackson, my research partner, and I had the privilege to work with a number of states when the research project developed to the point of dissemination of findings.

We were continually impressed with the dedication and expertise of the hunter education program personnel, both the Department of Natural Resource hunter education specialists and the volunteer instructors with whom they worked. They start the young or first time hunter off in the right direction, excited, having basic knowledge about gun handling, aware of hunter responsibility to fellow hunters and the non-hunter, responsibility to landowners and respect and honor to the animals that we hunt. We hunters need to follow up on the initial training so the young hunter can continue to develop into a dedicated, ethical sportsman. Our research documented that there was a major breakdown in the developmental process of becoming a hunter when the young, motivated hunter was not able to continue the development by having the opportunity to hunt with an ethical hunter who would take the time to teach him or her the way of the hunt.

I was taught to hunt by my Dad, and his first objective was to teach me how to shoot, then how to become a hunter. Two months after my ninth birthday, on a September day, he brought home my first gun. A used, five shot, Stevens bolt action 410 shotgun. I can remember the day, the time of day, and my excitement as well as his. He had two boxes of shells and we went out back of the barn, where he set up some cans and had me shoot. We kept up at the target practice until I could hit them every time, which I now realize was not a great feat of shooting, but it satisfied his expectation of my shooting ability.

The gun had to be cocked by hand or by raising and lowering the bolt, which I raised since it was too hard for me to pull the firing mechanism. I am left handed so I had to either take the gun from my shoulder or reach over the gun to cock, eject, or reload, so what I had in reality was a five shot single shot. I never asked him, but I think he had all of this figured out, as he was of the mindset that you take one shot and that shot should always do the job. Using semi-automatics did not fit his definition of hunting.

After he bought the first two boxes of shells, it became my responsibility to buy my own shells, and I can recall my personal debate about what size shell, two and three quarters or three inch to shoot. There was a price difference and two and three quarter won out.

The first frosts came in early October and my hunting lessons began. There was a good population of grouse and I could go any direction from the house and find old logging roads that were full of new clover, tag alders lining small creeks, swamps with highland ridges alongside or through them, highlands with patches of thick hazel brush, young poplar trees, and grouse everywhere.

Dad taught me to hunt the grouse. He took me out a few times and showed me the cover to look for, and then we would walk until we jumped a bird. He would watch its flight, then we would carefully walk to where he thought it would set down, and we would sit silently watching. After fifteen minutes or so the bird would usually start to cluck, raise its head to look around, and then start to walk. The grouse was ours.

At that time in my life, school was not of great importance to me. I put my time in and waited for the day to end so I could get home and get into the woods. Every night and every weekend I pursued the grouse. By the end of fall I knew their habitat, I knew their feeding habits, and I knew some of them by name because they would always get away from me, but some didn't.

I was learning to respect the bird's ability to get away and at the same time realized that to bring birds home required skill. There was a lot to know and it seemed like I had to keep learning as the habits and habitat changed as the season changed. This became the challenge and started to define the hunt. It was to study, to remember, to keep changing and adjusting, if I was to be successful with the harvest. I read every Outdoor Life and Field and Stream that I could get my hands on, listened to the local grouse hunters whenever I could get close enough to hear them, and continually thought grouse.

The snows came in December and my interest was then turned from grouse to snowshoe hares. My Dad's pulping business changed as the seasons changed and by early winter, the swamp would freeze and he and Grandpa then started to cut spruce and tamarack, both swamp trees. I would go with them every weekend. Dad would take time to go with me and point out cover and sometimes make short drives, and I started to become successful with the harvest. The only requirement of me was to use one shot per rabbit, report in at noon, have lunch, and be back by dark for the journey home.

We hunters must become involved with the future hunters. I was fortunate that Dad's livelihood and my introduction to hunting had perfect rhythm. Few young hunters of today have such an opportunity.

We have the responsibility to introduce young hunters to hunting and when we do, they need to be brought into the fraternity of hunters through a model of high legal and ethical standards. Our research documented that one of the factors that caused a hunter to evaluate his own ethics and then emulate high standards was when the model hunter was called "Dad" and was teaching his son or daughter. Over the past years, there have been many men who have shared their stories with me regarding the joys of having their son or daughter become their hunting partner. The highlight of their stories was when they would say how good and honest a hunter their son or daughter had become. I always asked them if they knew how the skills and ethics of their hunting partner had come to be, and the usual response was a smile and a positive headshake.

The American hunting tradition is the direct result of family values that have been handed down from generation to generation. Four out of every five hunters enter the world of hunting because they honor their family and want to be an important, contributing, and recognized member. During our interviews, fathers talked with passion and understanding about their sons and daughters; sons and daughters talked with respect and understanding of their fathers and siblings, the hunts and the hunting experience.

As our country developed, people lived primarily a rural existence, forcing the family to be a cohesive unit. Survival depended on it. The family worked together, played together, talked with each other, laughed and cried with each other as they intimately experienced life. The children were born in the home, the death and burial of family members took place at home, food was cooperatively gathered, preserved, and prepared at home, recreation and fun was programmed from the home, and every member of the family was an important contributor to the family's survival. Everyone was needed, and as each member fulfilled their roles and tasks, they became important and recognized, with respect for self and the family becoming the outcome.

Hunting was a significant part of the food gathering process, and the skilled hunter was an invaluable link in the survival process. As they harvested animals for food, their importance to the family was authentically recognized and they knew what it meant to be needed.

I was an adolescent in the 1940s and 50s and fortunate to be born into a family where I could be an integral part of the work ethic and contribute to the family income.

My Dad and Mom worked seven days a week, long hours, to make enough money to pay the bills and provide a home for us. When I turned twelve, I was able to start working in the woods with Dad. I would join him after school and on the weekends and work side by side as we cut pulpwood. I would never have thought of being paid for the work as the privilege to work with him and contribute to my family's income far out-weighed any need for pay.

As our society moved from a self-sustaining family pattern to one of dependence on others, our lifestyles significantly changed. As reliance upon mass production, affluence, mobility, technology, and non-participatory recreation became common, the opportunity for a young person to be a significant, contributing family worker decreased.

In my work as a counseling psychologist, I have worked with many clients who have been members of dysfunctional families. As they talked about their problems, they often came to the same conclusion: somewhere, at some time, they found themselves living in a time and place where they sensed they had little or no position of importance.

To be recognized and have had a position of importance in the family was basic to having a sense of well being about one's self. I have attempted to help many families find ways that will help their children have the feeling that they are needed as both a contributing member of the family as well as one that is honored and loved. In our present affluent, urban living pattern, at times it was difficult to find ways to legitimately provide the opportunities for children to have the needed family contributor position, which then often lead to over compensation by trying to buy the children's honor and love.

The hunting family is one of the places where the variable of contributor can be equalized with honor. When the hunting family talked about preparation for the hunt, as well as the hunt itself, the need to work as a team was often emphasized. During preparation for a hunt, the young hunter had specific responsibilities that were of absolute necessity for the hunt to be successful. They had to plan for food, clothing, footwear, gun or bow case, license secured, and specific packing for each trip. During the hunt, the young hunter again became a team member having to continually demonstrate responsibility of hunting safety, learning the woods, following directions, developing patience and fortitude, and continual alertness and problem solving. During the harvest of an animal, they had the personal feelings that come when a team goal is achieved, of being one of the members that was involved and needed for the outcome to be successful.

The time of the first harvested bird or animal was often an occasion for celebration that honored the individual accomplishment. During the in-depth home interviews, hunters often related their own experience, or their son/daughter's, of the first harvest of an animal and the family celebration.

I had the opportunity, on two occasions, to develop the hunting tradition with two of my own children, as our son Dan, and daughter, Sara, both indicated a desire to hunt whitetails. I did not do it right, and neither has become a hunter. I realize how I have missed an opportunity to have been with them, enjoyed the thrill of the hunt, worked together as a team, shared each other's successes, continually gotten to share and know them better, and to have a common interest and bond.

I should have known how to teach my children to hunt, because my dad had modeled the way. First, he modeled how to hunt by having me with him. I should have taught both Dan and Sara how to hunt by having them with me. The young hunter needs to be in the woods often with their dad prior to the season, learning the woods, the habits and habitat of the game, sensing the oneness between hunting partners, and having fun. There is nothing like time in the woods: the smells, the sunshine, the shadows, the changes, the colors, time to sit by a tree and have lunch, time to talk, time to know each other, time to build the tradition.

I did not take the time to share it with Dan and Sara. I took them out a week or so prior to the season and helped them find a stand that was fairly close to where I would be, then left them there on opening day. I checked on them every few hours, but I did not take the time from my own hunting to enjoy theirs, and I cheated them and myself. Dan hunted until he was eighteen and then started college, then his interests took him in a different direction. I did not prepare Sara at all. In fact, I spent almost no time with her to nurture her hunter interest. She had graduated from hunter education and was excited about the hunt, but I did not even spend time developing her shooting ability. Opening day of the whitetail season was cold, I had her on the top of a draw that came out of a marsh and worked its way up into a stand of hardwood. The wind would hit her and chill her to the bone. I was so insensitive and focused on my own hunting that I did not take the time to spend the day with her. I should have gotten her and gone into the hardwoods, built a fire to warm her, and we could have spent the day together. She stuck it out through the second day, returned to school on Monday, and has never hunted since.

When our kids tell us they want to become hunters, we have to alter our own hunting ways and for the rest of our lives have them become our purpose. First, we should teach them to connect with the woods, understand and respect the land, then to appreciate and know the ways of the animal that is being hunted, then the ways of the hunt. It takes a lifetime to do so.

We, as hunters, have the opportunity to become involved with young hunters as they complete their hunter education course. The hunter education instructors have given them the basics and we need to help them further their interest and begin to develop the tradition of hunting. We should take them into the woods, either on a one-on-one basis, or in small groups, and let them experience the woods as an experienced hunter does. Teach them to appreciate the land, its ability to sustain the habitat, how habitat related to animals' behavior, and how experience teaches one to become a hunter. When hunters train youngsters in the purpose of the hunt, the young hunter becomes identified with the ideal of becoming a life-long hunter. We have the opportunity. The future of hunting depends on it.

CHAPTER 2
THE DEVELOPMENTAL PLATEAUS

Before you read this chapter, take time to answer the following question. Write your responses in the space provided. Why do I hunt?

Assume there are no restrictions placed on you—you have no family, work, or financial restraints—and that you have one last hunt left in your lifetime. Describe that hunt.

Bob and I divided the workload of the research. Bob had the responsibility to direct the project by designing procedures of ethical research and to ensure that all data accumulated would be confidential so no individual could or would be identifiable once the data was recorded. He also contacted and met with individuals and organizations to obtain funding, to design and oversee the process of statistical analysis of the data, and to produce the manuals that would document the statistics.

My job was to design the observation and interview instruments, to field test them, to train the observers and interviewers to a significant level of proficiency; and to coordinate the observation and interviewing processes. We worked as partners in the interpretation of the data, the writing of professional articles, and the implementation of workshops for the dissemination of the findings.

The follow up interview, conducted in the home of the hunters and arranged after the hunters had been interviewed in the field following his/her hunt, was the primary instrument to determine the motivation that caused the hunter to hunt. I wrote the question, "why do you hunt?" as primary to probe the motivation issue. When field-testing the question, hunters found it difficult to answer, so we then added satisfaction-rating scales based upon information gleaned from hunters that we had met as we did the preliminary planning.

After conducting and analyzing about twenty-five interviews that had resulted from the open-ended questions and the rating scales, we became aware that there appeared to be patterns to the responses. We clustered the responses and after studying them, hypothesized that there were developmental stages or sequences that hunters progress through as their hunting world expanded over time and experience.

I then added a third question pertaining to motivation: "If you knew you only had one more hunting day in your lifetime, how would you spend it?" It became the question the produced the most evidence that hunters do evolve through developmental levels.

Psychologists who study life span development have documented the fact that we pass through stages as time evolves. The stages of childhood, pre-adolescent, adolescent, young adulthood, adulthood, middle-age, pre-retirement, retirement, and old age are well accepted.

The late Dr. Keillor Ross has documented stages of death and dying that people transcend when they have terminal illness: denial, bargaining with God for continued life, anger, acceptance, and peace.

Dr. Joyce Brothers has described five stages that men go through from twenty-one to death and how they impact upon marital relationships. From twenty-one to thirty-five, the onward and upward period, man is establishing himself in three areas of equal importance: marriage, work, and starting a family. During this period men, usually in their mid or late twenties, go through the make or break period where marriage and work can become major constraints causing pressure on the marriage and break-ups.

The late thirties, the consolidation period, is when he is satisfied and becomes settled in his work, family life, and marriage can prosper. If the opposite happens then there is more conflict.

During the forties, the pivotal decade, he realizes he is in middle age and may look for ways to recapture his youth, new jobs or divorce and remarriage to a younger woman. During the fifties, equilibrium stage, if the man has worked through the problems of the pivotal decade, the marriage can be very fulfilling. If he hasn't, it can be very difficult. Sixty-five years and on is the retirement stage and if he enters the stage with satisfaction of self, marriage can be very companionable and enjoyable; however, if the man isn't satisfied with himself, the opposite will happen.

Developmental stages are part of the process of change that brings one through the demands of everyday life. It leads to either a fulfilled maturity or one of non-fulfillment and then continual searching for meaning.

We were interested in trying to document why hunters quit hunting. Our major study focused on active hunters, but we did find and talk with some individuals that had been hunters and had stopped. The primary reason appeared to be physical, poor health being the number one reason. They stated that the physical demands of the hunt combined with elements of weather caused fatigue that became too much. Some mentioned that they had a physical injury, usually to the legs or shoulder, and hunting aggravated the condition, again causing them to quit.

We were interested to listening to the hunters who had quit because they no longer wanted to hunt. One of them related that he had started to hunt at the age of twelve, and had hunted whitetails consistently for the next forty years. He and two friends had purchased hunting land, built a hunting shack, been successful with the harvest, and that he had thoroughly enjoyed every aspect of the hunt.

He said he never regretted a moment of the various aspects of his hunting experience, yet he quit at the age of fifty-two. He said he was sitting in his stand, on an extremely cold November day, at eleven o'clock on Tuesday to be exact, waiting for his hunting partners to hunt through to him, when he decided he wasn't going to hunt anymore. They returned to the shack for the noon meal, and he said he told them he was done hunting. They laughed as they thought he was joking. After lunch he put his gun away and never hunted again. Most weren't as adamant about their decision to quit as he was, but the scenario was usually somewhat the same.

Bob Jackson and I spent hours trying to understand the reasons. Some of them focused on a life change that the individual had experienced. A number of them had become friends with men who were not hunters, oftentimes golfers, and their allegiance to hunting changed. Some stated that family and/or work responsibilities simply became so demanding, that something had to give, and it was hunting. Some just lost their interest.

As we analyzed different cases, it appeared to us that hunters, who choose to quit with other than health issues, were individuals who seldom became strongly committed to hunting even though they may have participated for a significant amount of time.

Consequently, they did not put the time, energy, and financial investment into the sport that would cause them to progress from the beginning developmental stages to one of the following sequential stages. The non-movement to the next developmental stage resulted in their loss of motivation.

We believe there are five stages that hunters can progress through or to: the shooter phase, the limiting out phase, the trophy phase, the methods phase, and the sportsman phase. It is important to understand that when we transcend from one stage to the next, the motivation of the prior stage continues and becomes incorporated into the present stage.

Shooter Stage

The hunters at the shooter stage consistently referred to two specific aspects as highlights of the hunt: the seeing of game and the opportunity to shoot at it. Seeing game was of equal importance to the infatuation with the gun or bow and the realization that it had the power to take game. Waterfowlers would talk, showing excitement when they referred to seeing large flights of birds or the moment they jumped a large flock of birds, that seemed to be getting up everywhere, followed with a lot of shooting. Seldom was the fact mentioned that they needed to hit the birds, but just having the chance to shoot at them appeared to be satisfying. A good or excellent day occurred when a box of shells had been shot, their shoulder was a bit tender, and they knew there would be birds available to shoot at the next day.

The whitetail hunters, though not getting a lot of shooting, were equally satisfied when they had seen a good buck, saw a large number of deer, or had seen a big buck and shot at it. The need to have harvested the buck was not as important as having seen it and taken a shot.

The wanting to see game aspect of the shooter phase stays with the hunter as a strong motivational force throughout their hunting career. Whenever hunters gather and talk hunting, there will always be a period in the conversation when they relate to each other times when they saw large numbers of game or trophy animals, and everyone listens and gets excited. The times when those ducks just kept coming, when they jumped and wave after wave kept getting up. When a number of whitetails came by and it seemed like the line wasn't going to stop, or when three or four bucks came by together, the excitement of seeing them overshadows the need to harvest. We want to hear about it.

I started to duck and whitetail hunt when I was twelve. I couldn't wait to get back to school on Monday morning to talk about the weekend hunt. All of us beginners talked about how many we had seen, seldom about how many we had gotten. Whoever had seen the most and shot the most shells held the status for the week.

Fred, my bow hunting partner, and I hunt the same area for whitetails. Fred and a colleague of his own a couple of hundred acres and an acquaintance of mine owns an adjoining couple hundred acres of wild land. Fred and his partner hunt on their land and I hunt the adjoining land, but Fred and I help each other put up stands so we know their placements and surroundings. Every evening after an individual day of hunting, much to my wife Carole's dismay, we get on the phone and discuss in detail every whitetail we had seen that day.

We hunt two entirely different areas for firearm season, yet we do the same thing.

We talk about how many we saw and all the details of when we saw them, the weather conditions, numbers of bucks, times of day, and the more we talk, the more excited and motivated we are to get out the next day. The seeing of game remains a high that never leaves us.

All of us who hunt have an infatuation with the gun or bow and are in awe of its power. To be able to master and control that power is a significant part of why we hunt.

We hunt to get the opportunity to shoot, and at the shooter stage, just the experience of pulling the trigger or releasing the bow is satisfying. I have duck hunted with a number of beginners and watched their expression of satisfaction as they emptied the gun and then stood watching the birds keep on flying. The fact that none fell made no difference.

I got my first buck during my third year of whitetail hunting. The first year, I missed three of them, the second year two - one a big old trophy and then, just minutes after daylight on the opening day of the third year - I finally got one. I shook no more and was no more excited on that one than the first five that I had missed. The shooter stage was very real for me.

At this stage, the shooting at a sought out live target became the factor that caused an excitement and high. The young hunter needs the opportunity to do a lot of shooting before they begin the experience of hunting, to be confident in their beginning mastery of their gun or bow, yet it will still be different when they shoot at the wild bird or whitetail for the first time. I am not sure the excitement and high ever goes away. I can remember my dad telling me that if the day came when he didn't sense the high after shooting a buck, he would stop hunting. He didn't stop.

The Limiting-Out Stage

The shooter stage was most often identified by beginning hunters who, when they responded to the hunter satisfaction scales, rated their hunts as very satisfying. During the interviews they expressed a high degree of enjoyment while hunting and indicated a high standard of ethical hunting behavior. (None of the developmental stages are an indicator of level of satisfaction or of unethical hunting behavior. In all of the stages, there were a few who showed disrespect to themselves by using hunting as a way to project their own selfishness. The majority enjoyed the hunt, had high ethical standards, and reported high levels of satisfaction after the hunt.)

Hunters view experience as their primary means by which they evaluate their own level of expertise. They ranked themselves through a self-rating scale as either novice, experienced, or expert. Seventy-five percent of the whitetail hunters rated themselves as experienced, twelve percent as novice, and twelve percent as expert. Sixty-eight percent based their self-rating on years of hunting experience. Seventy-two percent of the waterfowl hunters rated themselves as experienced, twenty percent as novice, and nine percent as expert. Fifty-six percent based their self-rating scale on years of experience.

Hunters realized that there was no substitute for experience when one was performing in the marsh or woods. You can learn about hunting from the books, but the only way to learn how to hunt was by doing it.

Experience caused most hunters to move from the shooter stage to the limiting-out stage. Some hunters reach a particular stage and even though they continued to hunt, they stayed at the same developmental stage, which we termed as plateauing. We interviewed a small number of hunters who had years of hunting experience, who described their last hunt and the reasons why they hunt in terms that depicted the shooter stage.

The limiting-out stage developed when the hunter's motivation changed from seeing game to getting game. He/she had enough hunting experience that hunting skills developed to a point where they knew how to read habitat and therefore knew where to hunt, they were more ready when a whitetail jumped or came through cover on the move, knew where there was a high probability of jumping waterfowl, and understood where and how to set decoys.

They moved through the woods or marsh in a more positive and determined way, looking ahead instead of at their feet. They realized when to slow down and watch, when to stop and wait, and when to move through and get out of marginal cover. They now get closer to the birds or whitetail, and the probability of taking game increases.

They have made a commitment to hunting and they have invested in better equipment, the old shotgun or rifle was replaced with new ones. Clothes that fit the person as well as the environment were purchased and new boots bought so the old hand-me-downs that were too tight, leaked, and were cold were gone. They were starting to feel comfortable in the woods or in the marsh. The fear of getting lost and not knowing how to get out has disappeared. Confidence in their ability to get game had increased. They now need to prove to themselves that they can produce.

Comfort level and confidence with the handling of the gun or bow had also increased. The gun now cradles in the arm and feels easier to carry. They no longer needed to check the safety every five minutes to make sure it was on; they knew they put it on at the start of the hunt and need only to check it occasionally. When the gun came up to the shoulder, the safety was off, it was in the right place, and they looked right down the barrel or through the scope. When it swung, it moved and kept on swinging as it followed the duck or whitetail. They have shot on the shooting range, and knew they could hit clays and put three holes in the bull's-eye at one hundred yards. They are confident and ready.

The limiting-out stage was logical. Wanting to get a limit of ducks, get three out of four, drop the running whitetail with a clean kill, or when conditions were right to take the long shot and have him drop, had become a reality. The hunt became purposeful and done in earnest. Satisfaction was measured in the taking of game.

The whitetail hunter began the hunting season with the purpose of putting venison on the table. If he/she hunted with a group, the plan was to fill every one's tag. The party or group hunt was indicative of the limiting-out stage.

During last year's firearm season, I was hunting the edge of a swamp, and as I moved slowly along, I heard a drive start to the south of me. I realized it was coming my way and I was in the middle. There was a creek bottom with open land to the north, and I realized the drive was being made to it. I decided to just stay put and let the drive go past, but one of the drivers came directly to me. He was a local hunter that I knew and the party he hunted with were hard hunters, had high ethics and were very successful at filling tags. They knew the land, had hunted it for years, and knew how the deer moved when driven. They had perfected the system.

I talked with him for a short while and he said on opening weekend they had shot ten bucks in their party of twelve. On Sunday night, when we took my grandson's doe to the ranger station to be registered, a party of ten was also registering their deer, and they had limited-out. One of their hunters was going from vehicle to vehicle telling everyone who would listen they had ten for ten. Limiting-out or filling the tag became the primary factor for hunting.

Waterfowl hunters, who were avid in their pursuit and invested heavily in expensive equipment, stated that water fowling was their favorite hunting, and told us that limiting-out was a major part of their expectation. When they didn't limit out, their personal satisfaction of the hunt was lowered.

Opening weekend water fowlers who get out a few more times and haven't set a high expectation for bagging birds, had the highest self-ratings of satisfaction for any single waterfowl hunt, as well as the entire waterfowl season.

Limiting-out can set oneself up for lower satisfaction, yet it was the stage where many hunters appeared to be. Data from the study indicated that forty-nine percent of the waterfowl hunters and thirty-five percent of the deer hunters were at the limiting-out, bagging game stage. I want to re-emphasize that whatever stage the hunter was at was not a factor which caused ethical or unethical hunting practices, nor is there any attempt to imply that hunters needed to move from stage to stage. Hunters who had a focus on getting game often demonstrate and exhibited the behaviors of an ethical hunter.

I have hunted for over fifty-eight years, starting at nine - limiting out and filling tags are still a major part of why I hunt. When I leave the truck in the morning and head for the marsh, I hunt to fill out a limit. When I start the bow and firearm season on whitetails, I plan on filling my tags and helping Oscar, Zack, and Wildon with theirs.

When I head west or south for a pheasant hunt, I plan on returning with the limit. The intensity to get game is as strong today as it was when I started my hunting pursuits.

When I was twelve I added duck and deer hunting to my pursuits of grouse and snowshoe hare. My dad's idea that hunting and harvesting should be done with one shot had a continual effect. I whitetail hunted with him, and, although he never said so, he must have wondered about my first five opportunities for whitetails, all misses.

He never hunted ducks, so I started them on my own, again trying to sneak up on them and make one shot do it all. I quickly realized that the four ten wouldn't do the job, so I made my first change of guns. My grandpa had an old single shot twelve gauge; it became my gun of desperation for the next two years. It kicked so hard that I had to put a small pillow under my coat to cushion my shoulder, but it had a close pattern and the grouse and rabbits seldom knew what hit them. I hunted ducks on small ponds and small creeks, always after mallards.

My first attempt to bag ducks was to shoot them on the water, and I soon realized that it was hard to kill them when they were setting or swimming, as most of the time I would get a b.b. or so in them, then had to spend the next hour or so looking for them. I observed that when they jumped there was a moment when they seemed to stop in flight. Wing shooting began.

I was still at the shooter stage, seeing the grouse, ducks, and hares and getting a chance to shoot was my greatest satisfaction, but bringing them home was becoming more and more important.

At fourteen, I bought my first two guns, both pumps and in good shape: a Westernfield twelve-gauge pump and a model 760 Remington .300 Savage. The potatoes growers in the area had a three-year crop rotation - one year being oats, followed by clover, then potatoes. There was a large population of sharp tails that stayed in or around the grain and clover fields, and I learned how to wing shoot on them. I expanded my duck hunting to include Bluebills, as there was a chain of lakes close to home that were connected by narrow waterways and the bills would use the waterways as their flyway from lake to lake. Mornings before school, I would set up on one of the waterways and pass shoot. By the time I was sixteen, I could hit flying birds fairly consistently, and the idea of limiting-out became real.

I shot my first limit of grouse fifty-one years ago. I was hunting the fringe of a large stand of white pines with open areas that had thick hazel brush growth. I was leaving a heavy cover area, and there was a large open area before the growth started again. Birds began to get up on my left. I picked the first one, and then followed up on four more. I remember the amazement of what had just happened as I picked up the five birds from the dead grass. For the rest of my hunting days limits were a major criteria of satisfaction.

When hunters told us about the limiting-out stage, they consistently mentioned that bagging game, coming together of their hunting skills, wanting to spend more and more time in the woods, continual confidence in their ability to hit what they were shooting at and the sense of comradeship with fellow hunters all combined to cause a multitude of satisfaction. The thrill and sense of accomplishment that went with being able to bag game became real.

The Trophy Stage

Hunting skills were perfected, and the ability to bag game had been proven to one's self as the hunter had harvested enough birds and whitetails to have reached a level of competency. Being able to harvest game was definitely a possibility, and selectivity became the motivator. The whitetail hunter talked of waiting for the big buck. They could easily pass up small and medium-sized bucks, even if it meant going without a filled tag as they now spent their hunting days after the big one. Waterfowl hunters also talked of selectivity as a limit of greenheads became more important than a mixed bag of birds. Small ducks like teal or ruddy ducks were passed over, hens were let go, and drakes became the more sought after prize.

The trophy whitetail hunter was the most interesting to listen to, as the possibility of taking the big buck was all consuming. They had done their research. They knew how the big bucks behaved, when times of solitude were expected, when and how the buck established dominance, and rituals of the breeding season. The firearm hunters hoped that the rut would coincide with the upcoming season..

Most of them had experienced the excitement and thrill of having seen a truly big buck during a hunt, and a number of them had already experienced the accomplishments of taking trophy animals. They had spent time talking to people that lived in particular areas, checked to see if any big bucks had been seen when involved in scouting. A number of them had changed hunting areas and were willing to travel distances to hunt areas that might produce a really big buck.

We asked them what defined a trophy buck. They responded antler spread, size, or configuration constituted the basic elements. When they talked spread, it was usually described as beyond the ears. Diameter was also used and often compared to the size of a person's wrist. A few hunters had seen a buck with unusual antler growth, such as down spikes or atypical points. It became their quest; it became their trophy.

Trophy hunters often stated that after they had shot enough whitetails there was no challenge in shooting small or average bucks. This interested us as we were continually looking for reasons that caused hunters to move from one stage to the next. We asked hunters what the number of kills was that caused them to move from limiting-out to the trophy stage.

There was no average number. It was an individual decision, and years of hunting appeared to be as significant as the number of whitetails shot.

One hunter had become a trophy seeker after shooting one animal over ten years. He stated that he just enjoyed the hunt and that he had made up his mind that he would shoot only big bucks. Some had shot over fifty animals before they made the decision to only hunt trophies. Number of animals shot was not a concrete reason which caused the hunter to enter the trophy stage.

We estimated that about twenty-five percent of both deer and waterfowl hunters were primarily motivated by the characteristics of the trophy stage. Hunters at this stage began to talk more about experiencing the total hunting environment, were more aware of aesthetics, of other birds, animals and a sense of being by one's self in solitude, were more at peace as they waited and watched. There was evidence that some hunters who were at the first two stages hunted with limited awareness of nature and the environment.

I personally have never been motivated by being a trophy hunter. I enjoy hunting with a partner who is at this stage and abide by his standards. My bow-hunting buddy, Fred, is in the trophy stage and has set his goal at eight points or better and over an eighteen inch spread. I hunt adjoining land, honor his position, and hunt by the same rules. Yet, there is just as much excitement and feeling of accomplishment when I shot a small buck or doe as when I shoot a trophy buck. I just don't shoot a small one in Fred's area.

The Method Stage

There was major shift in what was satisfying as hunters moved into the method stage. The stages of shooter, limiting-out, and trophy have their primary satisfactions centered on seeing and harvesting game. During the method stage, primary satisfactions switch to the hunt itself. The taking of game becomes secondary to the methods used in the hunt; they hunt for the hunt itself. Hunters at this stage discussed their hunting with an almost feverish intensity. They said that hunting was one of the most important aspects of their lives and discussed the let down feelings they experienced when the season was over.

A number of whitetail hunters would go to different states to extend hunting time as well as waterfowl hunters who would follow the flight south, always trying to get more time for the hunt. They said the desire to hunt was a significant part of their being.

They were constantly reading outdoor and hunting articles that gave them information on methods and techniques of hunting as well as browsing through hunting catalogs and hunting supply stores to keep abreast of equipment changes.

The hunters had specialized in both the game they hunted and how they accomplished the hunt. Most of them hunted a second species, but we were primarily interested with the one they defined as favorite. Twenty-one percent of the hunters we collected data on hunted ducks exclusively. Another thirty-nine percent said that waterfowl hunting was their preferred hunt. Of the whitetail hunters, ninety-two percent said whitetails were their preferred hunt. Only eight percent of the whitetail hunters also participated in waterfowl hunting.

The avid water fowler showed such a degree of enthusiasm for his hunting that the designed two hour in-home interview often extended to three hours or more and the second pot of coffee was consumed. There was a lot to talk about such things as being up before daylight, home after dark, overcoming bad weather, breaking ice at times, loading and unloading a boat, piling in decoys and teaching a few young ambitious labs or goldens to hunt with them instead of wanting to hunt by themselves.

The duck hunter had invested heavily in specialized equipment: a favorite gun, special shot, clothes, hip boots and waders, specialized camouflage boat, decoys, calls, and a good retriever. Over eighty percent had a specialized method of hunting, sixty-two percent decoyed and called, another ten percent jump shot and eight percent were exclusively callers.

When they talked about their duck hunting, talk always focused on the hunt, never on the bag. The decoyers and callers were the most animated. The decoyer had favorite blocks they would show us and explain in detail what made them so effective, how they would choose the location for the set, how layout was placed to utilize weather and wind, and first sight of birds. The calling, circling, caution and apprehension - then the turning of the ducks with the call; or times when everything was perfect and birds would be coming while they were still out setting the blocks, and the fact that birds always came right after a cup of coffee had been poured. They would relive the hunt right down to the last detail.

The caller often told of getting on a small pond or along a waterway in a marsh and waiting for flying birds that could be turned and then brought them in with perfected techniques. His excitement would elevate as he described the initial turn of the birds when they became interested in his call, and then working the birds on in. How the birds would be stretching their necks and looking, of when to call being as important as how to call, and knowing how determined the birds would get when they finally decided to come in. The perfection of the method was the satisfaction.

There was a tendency for the whitetail hunter to gravitate toward less group hunting and to perfect the hunt based upon a one-on-one with the animal or hunting with a single partner. Many expressed wanting to be associated with a party through sharing a hunting cabin or meeting and talking with buddies, but to be more alone during the actual hunt.

Closely tied to the individuality of the hunt was the desire to hunt on familiar land where there was a history that could be recalled. The return to the old familiar stand before daylight, the familiar sighting when a whitetail approached, the bothersome red squirrel who returned around nine o'clock, knowing the patterns and typical crossing routes of the deer, and the excitement and anticipation of the wait all overshadowed the actual moment of the kill. The feeling of being alone in the woods, and of knowing that the odds were in their favor if they stayed long enough because it had happened so many times before. The hunt became the motivator and satisfaction came from the total experience.

A number of the whitetail hunters also talked about their method of hunting being primarily the still hunt. They described how satisfying it was to be able to walk up on a whitetail in its natural surroundings. They related how experience had taught them how weather and wind direction affected bedding deer, how they would use the wind as they moved through an area, how they had to work hills and side hills to see bedded deer if they were to get a shot when the deer jumped and moved out. Of the need to have watched for traces and signs of deer in the area, for continual patience to move slowly and that feeling of accomplishment when they finally connected. The satisfaction from the method overpowered killing the whitetail.

During the method stage, hunters often moved to a style or use of equipment where a handicap was introduced. Some of the firearm hunters said they continued to hunt during the firearm season but told us the bow or black powder season was their preferred method of hunting. When asked why bow or black powder, we consistently heard the same responses. They wanted the challenge of hunting whitetails in a more natural surrounding where the animals moved by natural patterns, and by harvesting them with more primitive equipment thus allowing the whitetail an advantage. The actual killing of the animal was seldom mentioned; method was the motivator.

It was difficult to pinpoint exact numbers of those who were primarily motivated by the method stage. Waterfowl hunters outnumbered whitetail hunters at this stage.

We estimated that approximately twenty percent of the water fowlers and fifteen percent of the deer hunters were at this stage.

Hunters we talked to at this stage also reported the taking of game had caused the hunt to take on a more complete sense of satisfaction. A number of whitetail hunters felt the perfect season would be to hunt every day, see a lot of game, and be able to pick out the one animal most desired and shoot it the last half hour of the last day.

I identified with hunters at the method stage. I hunt for the hunt. Anticipation of the season is great for me: trout in spring, muskies in late spring, and woodcock in early September, ducks in late September, grouse or pheasant in October, whitetail with the bow in late October, whitetails with a firearm in November, and whitetails with the bow again in December. They keep me alive and waiting for the future. I experience feelings of being let down as each season comes to an end, but then anticipation for the next season brings me back up again. The time I dread most is late December and that day I know is my last day in the woods for that year. I stay until well after dark (to my family's dismay) and wait for the moon to give me light to come out, and I realize how fortunate I am to be a hunter, to live in a country that condones hunting where any person who chooses to can be a hunter, and to have a wife that understands my desire to hunt.

In my twenties, thirties, and forties I started hunting at daylight and ended at dark.

I have now come to the realization that I don't need to get up in the middle of the night to take game. Some days I start early but I'm also satisfied to start around eight and stay till dark. I find it hard to leave the marsh or woods in the daylight. I wish to be there and see the late movements of ducks as they settle in for the night, to see the whitetail or two pass right at dark, and then to stay a bit more and feel the night come. It's light; it's dark and only then am I ready to make my way back to the truck. It just seems to me that part of the hunt is coming out after dark

I enjoy all of my hunting and it is almost impossible to pick out a preference, but if I had to it would be bow hunting. The totality of the hunt is what draws me. I hunt the same land year after year, place my stands in the same general area, and see the same gray squirrel, know when the robins will migrate through, when the nuthatches will appear, listen for the migrating swans and Canadian honkers and watch them fly overhead, see the landscape change from day to day as the leaves fall. I do my most personal and best thinking as I sit in the stand twenty-five feet up in the tree, and wait for the animal I choose to take. The hunt calls me back, day after day, and year after year.

The hunting season I appreciate most is the whitetail firearm season as I return to my original home area. I stay with my mother in her home and hunt the land that I grew up on, started my hunting on, where I worked side by side with my dad cutting pulp wood, hunted the whitetails with him, and have hunted the past fifty-eight years with my buddy Oscar. There is many an experience to recall and many a whitetail that has been dragged out of those woods.

Oscar and I, and now my two grandsons, Zack and Wildon, hunt the first two days together, and then the boys have to return to school. Zack is in college now, Wildon in his last year of high school. Oscar returns to his teaching profession. So I hunt alone until noon on Wednesday, and then take my mother home to our place in southern Wisconsin for Thanksgiving. I then return on Friday for the remainder of the season. I enjoy the entire season, but the two and one half days when I'm alone hold special meaning for me. I start around eight and still hunt until three then get in my stand until dark. From eight until three I walk the land that holds my memories and evaluate the satisfactions of the day's hunt by how many whitetails I can walk upon and catch in their beds. I sit on the same side hill each season for a couple of hours and look out over the marsh and creek bed to a small island where dad and

I cut pulp and where he shot his last whitetail. I think about him and wish he would be able to be with my wife Carole and me, my adult children, and his great grandchildren, and I give him honor. Hunting for the experienced hunter is not the killing of the game; it is to embrace the moments and recall the memories of past hunts.

The Sportsman Stage

We knew there was a final stage. Some veteran hunters told us about a stage where the satisfaction of having hunted was all that was necessary. We misnamed it - the sportsman stage, as sportsmanship should be an integral part of every stage. I was reading the March 1996 issue of Field and Stream and Gene Hill, as only Gene Hill could write it, named and typified the stage that seemed to be so illusive to name. The article was titled "choices" and focused on "No, I don't have to do this anymore." He then pointed out, "Unless I want to". He listed the things he doesn't need to worry about now that he has reached the "certain age":

I don't have to stay up until the fat duck hunter sings.

I don't have to wade through that to get there.

I can admit that I see most things before I hear them.

When offered a second helping of apple pie I can say, "why not?!"

I don't have to listen to a twenty-year-old guide tell me

where to climb something high and steep because there might be an elk there.

I can admire someone else's 28-gauge double and not commit the sin of envy.

I am not obligated to stay up all night before deer season and sleep all day in my stand.

I don't have to be the first on the water and the last off.

I don't have to sit in the duck blind past sunset and walk out in the dark, though I can if I want to.

I can say that I believe a woodcock in the bush is worth two in the hand.

I won't buy a new magic material fly rod until I figure out what happened to the magic in the old one.

I can face the fact that I won't ever be one of the legends of duck and dove shooting (I was born to be one but something went wrong).

I don't have to ride a horse with a wild eye or a name like Widow maker.

I can wear plain old clothes instead of "outfits".

I don't have to stop in every fly shop and buy a half a dozen of something I already have a dozen of. But I probably will.

I can let a cock pheasant bluff me into not shooting and like it.

I'll admit that I don't need a new 20 gauge. I'll even admit I didn't need the last one.

The stage was only reached by the dedicated who continued to hunt, but no longer needed to prove anything to self or others. We did not meet a lot of them, about five percent, but when we did it was a pleasure. They all had close to forty years - and some a lot more - of hunting experience. They had lived the good and bad experiences while out in the field, but the good was what was now recalled and told.

When we interviewed them, two factors stood out, their dedication to hunting and their deep respect for the game they hunted. Each one told us how hunting had affected his life, and each knew he or she was a more complete and contented person because of the hunt. They were the tradition of hunting.

To have hunters feel free to talk to us, we guaranteed them total confidentiality. We assured them they would never be identified by what they said and we would not directly quote them.

However, I am going to quote from one of the hunters that was in the "No, I don't have to do it unless I want to" stage. He was a dedicated duck hunter who had just finished his fiftieth year. I am confident that he cannot be identified by anyone else, but if he reads this and identifies himself, I hope he will not be offended:

> Once it was necessary for me to fill a gunny sack full to feel really good, but now it's different. Now it's

important to be in the marsh before daylight. I want to smell, hear, and really see the day break. I watch the frost melt off the reeds. I hear and see the morning flight as I warm my hands around a hot cup of coffee. I really don't have to shoot any more of those birds to have a good day.

I knew the marsh like the back of my hand. But I never would have been what I am today if I couldn't have been a hunter. Once each year, for the last ten years, I take the dog and go to the marsh at sundown. I spend the night. I put up a lean-to by some oaks, make a fire and late at night, after I had some time to think, I crawl into my sleeping bag and wait for the morning, and daylight. You know, I might not be around for the next season.

One of the firearm seasons I was not able to return to the north for the last days of the season. I hunted on some state-owned land close to home instead. On the last day, I was hunting some unfamiliar land and got turned around and wasn't sure of where I was.

I came out on a logging road, didn't know which way to go to get back to the truck, and then spotted an old pick up truck. It had a homemade camper on it, and I walked over to it. As I got near the truck, this voice said, "you lost?"

He came around the truck dressed in black wool breeches, black and red wool shirt, red suspenders, an old red wool cap, and I knew it was okay to tell him I was lost. I asked him if it would be all right to talk with him for a while. He was completing his seventy-first year of whitetail hunting. He said he used to go north on the train, stay in a tent with his buddies, and told me of some of the bucks they had shot. They cooked on an old barrel stove that they had built and left in the woods year after year. He told of how he saw the deer heard expand to southern Wisconsin, showed me his 38-40 octagon barrel Winchester, and explained how the rifle really did still shoot.

I asked him if he had gotten a deer, and he said, "no." I then asked if he would shoot one if he saw it later that afternoon. He said he really didn't know if he would, he would have to decide if one came by. He told me by his maturity, self-assurance, mannerisms, wit, and approach towards hunting that, "No, I really don't have to be out here, but I am because I want to be."

When the hunters of this stage planned and talked about their last hunt, none emphasized the taking of game. They usually returned to the place that had special memories, often memories related to the land or marsh that was familiar, land they hunted on when they were young, or land they presently or in the past owned. They would walk the land, or set out the decoys, or get in their stand, and almost always had ducks flying or coming in or whitetails being seen. They seldom had another person hunting with them. They were more focused on their personal involvement in the hunt and the recreation of a favorite day. None went to a new hunting area to shoot game, few even fired their gun.

Dad was moving into this stage, when at sixty, he had an unexpected and fatal heart attack. One cold opening morning of the firearm season, at about ten o'clock, I went to the island to have a cup of coffee with him. He had not shot, so I assumed no bucks had shown up. When I got there he had the familiar smile of having gotten one, and I asked him if he had seen anything. He pointed to a patch of tag alders, about sixty yards away, and told me how he had watched a fork horn stand there and look at him. I couldn't believe what I was hearing, I asked him, "Why didn't you shoot it?". He just said, "I really didn't want to." I understand now.

A second incident that I couldn't understand happened a year later. On Thanksgiving morning he had shot a buck that would satisfy most anyone in the trophy stage. We got the buck to his house around noon, got it hung up and went in for lunch. I was ready to go out again right after eating, and I assumed he was also, but he just stayed at the table. I said, "lets get going." and to my astonishment, he said he was going to stay home and watch his beloved Packers on television. I said, "Your going to do what?" He said, "No, I really don't have to go this afternoon. I want to watch the Packers."

I wonder if I will ever get to this stage?

Please go back and read your explanation of why you hunt and the description of your last hunt. Ask yourself which stage you are in, and when you know, your next hunt will have added satisfaction as you set your expectations from the stage you are in.

CHAPTER 3
THE ETHICAL HUNTER

How do you personally define the ethical hunter? Jot down your definition and then compare it to the definitions by hunters who were interviewed during the research.

Hunters, how do you distinguish the ethical hunter from the slob hunter? To see the two walking side by side down an old logging road, it would be impossible to pick out the two different individuals. It would probably be hard to tell the difference when you had a short conversation with them in the woods or on the marsh. However, if you had the opportunity to listen for a longer time, you would begin to sort them out, and if you could observe them hunting, you would definitely know.

When ethical hunters talked about hunting, you could hear their commitment to the sport, their deep and keen sense of the woods or wetlands, the thrill of the pursuit of the game, the perfection of the skills of hunting, their depth of knowledge of the game they pursue, and the joy that comes when experiences are recalled.

When unethical hunters talk, they quickly identify themselves. They express a strong dislike for the Department of Natural Resources and always know more than the game managers about the size of the deer herd or about the duck population. They know how to manage the resources far better than those college-trained department people do. They never have the chance to shoot as many ducks as the people do down the river; steel shot is bad, and wardens are the lowest of all life forms. They show their arrogance by expressing a selfish goal of the hunt. Much of their information about wildlife is based on folklore that has long been disproved. A short time into the conversation they are telling of their progress as a hunter by expounding on their shooting ability and expertise to take trophy animals or limit of ducks. Most of them like to talk, seldom listen, and have the answer to all the questions about wildlife management, guns, shooting, and harvesting game.

We listened to hunters and continued to study our data to determine how hunters themselves defined the ethical hunter. As the study progressed, we saw their definition form and then solidify by sheer numbers of references. Hunters defined the ethical hunter in terms of respect and exemplified practices that honored the land, the landowner, the non-hunter, fellow hunters, and the game hunted.

They stated that the ethical hunter always abides by the law and always demonstrates safe gun and hunting practices. They also expressed strong negative feelings toward violators and categorized them as the most unethical. The issues of violators are addressed in a separate chapter.

The Ethical Hunter Respects the Land

To harvest whitetails hunters need know two things: where they feed and where they bed. To harvest birds, it is basically the same: where and what they eat, their movements as the day progressed, where they roost or settle down for the night, what promotes their movement patterns from area to area, and how weather impacts their behavior.

Hunters expounded upon the fact that it was the land that produced the game. Without access, hunting stops. They related that an ethical hunter must become a student of the land. The more they learned, the more they realized there was to learn. Their knowledge base must continue to develop by reading, talking with fellow hunters, watching hunting videos, and continually returning to the land where they eventually became one with the land. They needed to develop a thorough knowledge of the vegetation of the land and what animals were most likely to feed on, the lay of the land and how it affected animal movement. How the season, temperature, weather conditions, and wind affect animal behavior. They reached their optimum knowledge of the land or marsh when they could predict where the whitetail or birds would be, instead of being surprised when they appeared.

One hunter explained his connection to the land by stating that he had hunted the same area for whitetails over the past fifty-six years, and only missed being on the land two years while in the Army and two years when he hunted an area in the Southwestern part of Wisconsin. He stated that the land called him back every year, as it was full of experiences that he needed to recall each year, it changed a bit, and he needed to be part of that change. Although it changed there was also a constant that didn't change, which he also needed.

Oscar, my rifle hunting partner, and I can identify with this hunter as we have spent the last fifty-six years hunting the same land. We know every hill, every valley, every turn the creek makes, every tag alder swamp, every spruce stand, and every poplar ridge.

We live to return year after year. We have also hunted ducks for the past forty-four years. We started our duck hunting by canoeing creeks and walking the marshlands, decoying on beaver ponds, and open water decoying when the northern flights were coming through. Eventually, jump shooting along creeks and marsh ponds became most rewarding and more and more time was spent in pursuit. It drew us back to the same one hundred and thirty acres of wetlands, and we started to know and connect with the land. We knew where each pond was, how and where the creek flowed, where the cattails grew, where the tag alders ran, where the oaks were, where the early season Teal, Woodies, and Mallards would be. When the northern mallards would come, we knew where they would congregate. We would meet at the same oak ridge for a morning cup of coffee and return for a sandwich at noon. We got to know the marsh and became a part of it. To experience the marsh became as satisfying as the taking of the birds.

The ethical hunter appreciated the land with a sense of awe and oneness and was part of the land, not separated from it. When one is truly part of something, they will not harm it by misuse, neglect, selfishness, or anger. Instead, they will protect it, nurture it, take pride in it, and relish the time spent with it.

The Ethical Hunter Respects the Landowner

Hunters need to respect the land they hunt on and respect the landowner, be they private individuals, corporations, or government. When land was self-owned, the owner expressed a deep respect and pride in it, and it was this respect and pride that hunters need to exemplify when they are on land owned by someone else.

One aspect of our research project was to document landowner - hunter relationships. The following checklist, along with hunter and landowner interviews were used to gather data about these relationships. The numbers on the following checklist are average responses from two hundred deer bow hunters pertaining to bow hunting and four hundred nine deer gun hunters pertaining to gun hunting. The ratings were collected from hunters who attended pre-season hunting clinics sponsored by local sportsman clubs or the Wisconsin Department of Natural Resources. The respective respondents completed a problem checklist consisting of nine items pertaining to bow hunting and eleven items pertaining to gun deer hunting that were identified as potential problem areas by hunters. One hundred twenty state game wardens, and fifty-one state game managers, as well as one hundred six landowners responded to the same checklist.

In the checklist, number one indicates greatest importance with number nine representing the least importance (one to eleven in the gun-hunting survey). Each of the four groups independently ranked the checklist items.

Hunter Problem Checklist - Deer/Bow Hunting

	Bow Hunters	Game Managers	Wardens	Landowners
Improper preparations (mismatched equipment, dull broad heads, etc.)	1	7	9	9
Failure to seek permission from landowners	2	4	4	1
Failure in skill (or effort) to make adequate retrieval of wounded deer	3	3	3	3
Lack of practice and poor marksmanship	4	6	6	4
Taking shots beyond effective range	5	2	5	2
Use of alcohol while or around hunting	6	9	8	7
Taking more than one deer per season	7	5	2	6
Hunting before or after hours	8	1	1	5
Hunting in large parties	9	8	7	8

Hunter Problem Checklist - Deer/Gun Hunting

	Gun Hunters	Game Managers	Wardens	Landowners
Poaching (out of season, nights, etc.)	1	2	1	2
Indiscriminate shooting	2	4	9	9
Hunting accidents, unsafe gun handling	3	6	4	10
Shooting illegal deer and letting them lay	4	3	6	6
Use of alcohol while or around hunting	5	5	7	8
Failure to seek permission from landowners	6	1	2	1
Failure in skill (or effort) to make adequate retrieval of wounded deer	7	10	11	11
Lack of practice and poor marksmanship	8	8	10	7
Taking more than one deer per season (using tags of non-hunters, children, etc,)	9	7	5	3
Hunting in large parties (10 or more)	10	9	8	5
Group bag (hunting for party)	11	11	3	4

Landowners rated not asking permission to hunt on private land as the greatest problem facing both bow and gun hunting. Bow hunters rated it as the second major problem facing bow hunting. Game managers and wardens ranked it as the fourth greatest problem facing bow hunting. When ranking gun hunting, both landowners and game managers ranked failure to seek permission from landowners to hunt on their property as the greatest problem facing gun hunting. Game wardens ranked it second. Gun hunters rated it as having a rank of six, perceiving it as not significant.

The rating scale aspect of the study was followed by randomly contacting one hundred six landowners from plat maps that statistically sampled the state of Wisconsin. We trained interviewers to conduct in home interviews with the landowners, before and after the gun-hunting season. Landowners were asked to keep a daily log as they observed hunters on their land during the entire nine-day rifle-hunting season. Landowner's logs reported that fifty-eight percent saw hunters on their land without permission; forty-seven percent recorded property damage or legal violations.

The two most recorded legal violations were shooting before or after hunting hours, followed by shooting from a roadway. Hunting on private land without permission is illegal, but we separated it for interpretation and reporting.

The follow up interview was designed to ascertain what landowner's major concerns were regarding hunter behavior. The five factors that were of most concern to landowners were, in order: not asking permission to hunt, property damage (field, crops, fences, cutting trees), shooting close to livestock or buildings, persistent trespassing, and illegal kill.

Landowners stated that they wanted to know who was on

their land; so asking permission was of absolute necessity. We asked hunters why they did not ask landowners for permission to hunt. The following reasons, in order of frequency, were reported: fear of rejection resulting in not gaining permission; pressed for time; difficulty in determining who owned the land or where the landowners may be located; following wounded game; and the conviction that game belonged to everyone and land not being actively farmed or used by the landowners was a "commons" and open to hunting.

Hunter involvement with landowners was the key to having land being made available for hunting. Three basic rules that must be adhered to are: always ask for permission, when given permission respect the land and the landowner when you are on their land, and do not violate. Involvement with landowners, and in particular with farmers, has the potential to go beyond the basic three. We often heard from farmers,

"They come and ask to hunt, but they never come and ask if they could help out by giving some of their time during the non-hunting season". A number of hunters had related to us that they were involved in more than just hunting. One in particular told us how he helped during spring planting, another helped with cutting firewood and the list should go on.

Local sportsman groups had a strong, positive influence on landowner-hunter relationships when they were involved in local conservation projects, oftentimes implemented on landowner's property. Habitat involvement projects, stream improvement, hiking trails, and bird watching areas all improved landowner's and the general public's image of hunting and hunters.

Our research documented that different areas of the state had significantly different attitudes regarding hunters and policies on posting. The area that had the most positive landowner-hunter relationships had the least posting. Positive attitudes stemmed from the strength of a rod and gun club in the region and the healthy relationships it nourished between the landowners and hunters. This sportsmen's group reared pheasants and released them on individual area farms. However, the relationship went deeper than that. The group traditionally had a long history of involvement in conservation activities. The club had a long history of vigor and activity. Interviews with our research team consistently heard landowners talk of their respect and appreciation for the activities of their club.

Some of the clubs had made leasing arrangements for hunting with landowners. This created an additional incentive for club membership, and reduced landowner anxiety because the landowners knew that the clubs would attempt to take responsibility for the behavior of hunters when they were on their land.

A third factor contributing to the positive landowner-hunter relationship was the result of the philosophy and work of the local game warden. When the warden was highly involved in the clubs as well as continually building community involvement, the outcome was demonstrated through positive hunter-landowner relationships. When wardens nurtured relationships in schools, 4-H clubs, sportsmen's clubs, or wherever the opportunity arose, hunters benefited by non-posting policies. The area with the most favorable hunter-landowner relationships and the least amount of posting had such a warden. He was the major influence that resulted in the local sportsmen club purchasing a large tract of land for public hunting. During interviews with this warden, he stated that his job was as much education as enforcement.

Ethical hunters sought permission to hunt by asking for the privilege well before the season. They checked again by phone or in person as the season approached and re-contacted the landowner to get permission to hunt if there was any change of numbers of hunters or time alterations after the initial understanding. They treated the land with total respect while hunting, and showed appreciation by volunteering to help the landowner or giving a special gift after the hunting season was over.

Landowners perceived ethical violations as more significant than legal violations. Stories of driving on planted crops, leaving gates open, parking in areas that made it impossible to move machinery from field to field, cutting of fences, shooting in livestock areas, bullet holes in buildings, and the disrespect they felt when hunters argued with them when they were told to leave the land, were all significant concerns of landowners.

If we plan to have the privilege to continue to hunt private land, we must get into the habit of always asking permission. Data from the research documented that but forty-two percent of hunters stated they asked landowners for permission to hunt. When asked why they didn't ask, the two most common responses were that they were afraid of being turned down or they didn't know where the landowner lived. Hunters cannot afford to legally or ethically violate the laws and standards of responsible hunting practices. If landowner's rights aren't considered, less and less hunting land will be available.

As the final phase of the landowner study, we had graduate students call a hundred landowners that represented a statistically correct state of Wisconsin representation. They collected data relating to the landowner's practice of granting permission for hunting over the last ten years. Seventy-seven percent stated that their practice had become more restrictive by posting for trespassing and/or allowing less hunter participation by restricting who and how many might hunt on their land.

The Ethical Hunter Respects the Non-Hunter

Hunters must address their relationship and responsibility to non-hunters. They hold the significant card to hunting's future. How well hunters answer their questions, inform them of their hunting heritage, discuss how important hunting is personally, and present a thoughtful and informed image, will determine if they will support the hunter's position or move to the anti-hunting sentiment. Sometime in the future hunting will become a political issue, and it will be used by politicians for votes. Which side has the greatest number—the hunter or anti-hunter—is how representation will be decided.

The hunter and the anti-hunter are in defined opposed positions, but the majority of the population makes up the non-hunter group, which has no significant allegiance to either side. Over time, they will move to support one side or the other. Hunters need to be sure it is their side. Seldom will a hunter trying to convince an anti-hunter of his/her rights to hunt be successful: nor will an anti-hunter convince a hunter to stop hunting.

Hunters need to keep themselves well informed as to the strength and strategies of the anti-hunter as they try to weaken the right to hunt and own guns. Hunters need to support local, state, and national organizations that counteract attempts to deny constitutional as well as heritage rights.

We conducted approximately 120 one-on-one interviews

with non-hunters to attempt to ascertain their questions and/or concerns regarding hunters and hunting. We identified the non-hunter as a person that had no prior relationship to a hunter. If they had a parent, relative or friend that had been a hunter, they were not chosen for an interview.

Each interview began with general questions about hunters and hunting. It was obvious non-hunters had not engaged in thinking or analyzing either. After we probed into their non-hunting world, the interviews would change direction and we asked them what questions they had regarding hunters and/or hunting.

Their first question was usually, "How can you kill a bird or animal?" This question was immediately followed by, "How does the hunter feel right after killing something?"

Realizing their most often asked questions were about the killing of game, we included a question on the hunter's immediate feelings after killing a bird or whitetail in the one-on-one home interviews.

Seventy-eight percent of the duck hunters related a feeling of either success or thrill. They used words such as accomplishment, competence, excited, elated, and exhilarated. Thirty percent of the bow hunters reported they felt nothing. Another twenty-six percent said they felt part of the balanced population aspect of an overall deer management plan.

We then asked the bow hunters a follow-up question. "On what basis would you explain or defend hunting and the taking of game to a non-hunter?" Sixty percent stated hunting and killing game is part of an overall game management plan. Another twenty percent said they would use the rationale that hunting is a sport.

Two percent of the duck hunters and three percent of the

bow hunters reported that they felt bad right after a kill. We interpreted this to mean they felt empathy for the animal. We concluded that the primary concern of the non-hunter centered on the issue of feeling empathy for animals. Therefore, the data indicates that the hunter and the non-hunter are at significantly opposing positions on this issue.

I believe the non-hunter group needs to be of concern to hunters. They could be easily swayed by anti-hunting and animal rights groups. They were typically individuals who had not experienced a bonding to the land, to the realities of nature, and had minimal experience with animals in their natural setting. They live a lifestyle where they have sheltered themselves from the reality of animals being raised for human consumption. They are seemingly oblivious or deny the fact of slaughterhouses and meat packing plants that put meat in supermarkets.

Attempting to explain hunting to them was like trying to explain something in a vacuum. Yet they could identify with animal rights propaganda and become anti-hunting advocates.

One way to avoid this kind of thinking and mindset is to have young minds educated correctly by understanding the concept of food chains and the ways that nature balances the ecosystem. Children who grow up and never have the opportunity to experience nature in a realistic way, become adults that are oblivious to the fact that animal survival depends upon food chains, the strong prevail, the weak die.

Hunters need to become very proactive and educate the non-hunting population of the positive outcomes that hunting provides for everyone. Hunters need to spread the word about the 1937 bill sponsored by Senators Pittman and Robertson and signed into law that designates an excise tax on guns and ammunition be established and the funds distributed amongst the states for wildlife habitat development projects and hunter education programs. Since 1937, hunters and target shooters have contributed billions of dollars to state wildlife restoration and hunter education programs. Senators Dingell and Johnson also sponsored a bill that became law that added an excise tax on fishing equipment, electric trolling motors, and sonar fish finders. The funds from this source of revenue also contribute millions of dollars for the benefit of fish habitat and environmental improvements. American sportsmen, by paying the two excise taxes, have contributed billions of dollars to states for fish and wildlife improvement programs.

Hunters promote and advocate for the employment of wildlife managers who manage for totally balanced ecosystems with population of plants, songbirds, and natural balance of animals that creates a food chain. This, in turn, creates an environment that is appreciated by bird watchers, amateur biologists, wild flower enthusiasts, nature observers, hikers, and photographers.

Hunters are well informed on the numbers and health of various species of birds and animals that are hunted and work cooperatively with various state organizations to set limits and seasons that will guarantee a strong, healthy future for each of the species. Hunters are a viable part of the local, state, and national economy as they purchase equipment that provide jobs in the workplace, income from travel and lodging, and revenue from the sales of licenses and specialized hunting stamps for specific species. We are in no way an enemy of animal populations or a social or economical drag, but are instead just the opposite.

An important non-hunter group is our marriage partners,

and, because hunting was predominately a male venture, the spouses were most often wives. What questions did they ask? They were aware of hunting and hunters and that hunting can become an activity that was extremely timely, expensive, energy consuming, and could cause a major conflict in a marriage.

We became aware of the seriousness of this conflict when we interviewed hunters and hunting groups. We interviewed a bow hunter club with a membership of eighteen. Sixteen of them were divorced and when we inquired as to this high rate, we were told that their dedication to hunting was one of the main factors for some of the break-ups. We then designed an inquiry to attempt to find out hunters' wives questions and perceptions regarding hunting. How did husband-wife teams find solutions when problems that pertained to hunting emerged? We put an ad in the local paper inviting hunters' wives to meet with us and help us assess the impact hunting had on their marriage. Eleven women responded to the ad, and we met for two-hour sessions, bimonthly, for three months.

What were their questions? The overriding one was, "why were they made to feel that they were excluded?" Hunters had stated that their wives were not interested in their hunting, and when they tried to tell them about their experiences, they weren't listened to. Obviously, a communication gap existed.

Two of the women had a hunter-hunter relationship with their husbands and stated that hunting was a significantly positive force that solidified the marriage. The rest had a relationship that when the husband hunted they had to find their own things to do, yet were expected to take care of the children and run the household in his absence.

As we talked and listened to the wives, it became apparent that there were significant differences in how they perceived hunting and hunters based upon the intensity of their husband's involvement. It appeared that the more intense the involvement, the more separation, the greater the resentment.

These women defined hunters by placing them in one of two categories: minimally involved or intensely involved. They defined the minimally involved as those who most often hunted a single species, whitetails as an example, on opening weekend and one or two days over the Thanksgiving weekend. If they hunted a second species, the time commitment was minimal.

Those who had a husband who fit the minimally involved category stated that they realized the importance hunting had for their husband. It was expected that they find someone to help out with the children while the husband was away if they wanted to spend time with their own friends or enjoy the time as they wished. They also said they would often spend time together as a family after the weekend was over, like going on a weekend trip, to make up for his being absent during the hunting season. They kidded about the special time after the hunt and said they thought it was planned because their husbands felt guilty about being gone. They appeared to have found compromising strategies and hunting posed no real threat or significant separation in their marriage. They did feel their husbands kept hunting primarily to himself or only shared it with his hunting partners, but were able to accept the feelings of exclusion, as it was not a major thrust that lasted over a long period.

The wives that were in a marriage with an intensely involved hunter related a different story. He started hunting in early fall and as the different seasons opened, he entered them all, and was absent a considerable amount of time over four months or more. They also related that when he wasn't hunting, they would sense a feeling that he would rather be hunting than at home. During the early years of their marriage, it did not pose as much of a problem as they did not have families and could find things to do that were need fulfilling. When the children were born, it became a major problem as they lost their sense of freedom due to needed child care. Yet, he continued to have his freedom, and they became resentful. They felt exclusion and their major question became, "why doesn't he feel satisfied? He can get a limit of ducks one day and yet he is just as motivated to return the next day." One wife said, "How many ducks, geese, pheasants, and deer does he have to shoot to feel he is ready to quit?"

We asked them if they had ideas for solutions to the separation they were experiencing, and they stated they did not. One woman related this was one of the factors resulting in divorce for a friend of hers. Two other women joked and said they thought it would get better when he got so old that he would not have the strength to keep going at his present level.

Each of us who hunt fall somewhere on a continuum of minimal involvement to maximum involvement. From listening to the women, it is obvious we need to be sensitive to our partners and be willing to talk with them about their feelings and perceptions of hunting and to try to help them understand our wanting to hunt. It is our responsibility to initiate conversation and to work towards understandings that allow each to have feelings of fulfillment and contentment. Compromise can only happen when there is communication.

To ensure the future of hunting, hunters need to become aware and involved with the various non-hunter populations. We are in competition with anti-hunters for the support of the non-hunters.

The Ethical Hunter Respects Fellow Hunters

During post-season one-on-one interview sessions with four hundred-seventeen duck hunters and two hundred fifty-eight deer hunters, each hunter was asked, "What has been your most dissatisfying experience as a hunter?" The following percentages reflect their responses regarding hunter-to-hunter behavior.

Seventy percent of duck hunters reported that their most dissatisfying experience pertained to the hunting behavior of another hunter. They related incidents of shooting before and after legal hours, hunters taking birds they had not shot, dogs out of control, sky busting, crowding, arguing over use of blinds and possession of dead ducks.

Eighteen percent of the firearm hunters related that hunter-to-hunter behavior was their most dissatisfying experience. They related examples of crowding, indiscriminate shooting, and disagreement over the tagging of a deer and observation of large hunting parties.

Seven percent of bow hunters related that fellow hunter-to-hunter behavior was the factor that caused them the most dissatisfying experience. When questioned more, these bow hunters seldom related in-field, direct hunter-to-hunter behavior, but instead focused on fellow hunters who used outdated, poorly kept equipment, who took unreasonable shots, bragged about wounded deer that were not retrieved, and disrespect of landowner rights.

By nature, hunters are not disrespectful of fellow hunters. A congested area where a hunt took place was paramount to the problem. Waterfowl hunting, along firing lines that border refuges, was where hunters reported the largest amount of insensitivity. Public hunting grounds where pheasants were planted was second, and public hunting grounds that draw large numbers of deer hunters came in third.

Crowding was the number one factor that caused hunter-to-hunter disrespect. When the hunting environment was of limited space, game congregated in specific areas. Ducks follow flight patterns and routes as they come and go from the refuge; pheasants stayed close to their release areas. Whitetails were hunted on state-owned land that had a high deer per square mile count that resulted in a high hunter concentration. Deer hunters said they would find a stand, get set, and then someone else would move in on their position. When the hunt was on public land, no one had legal jurisdiction to a spot, so the only means of regulating the area was by a fellow hunter respecting the space of another.

The second most reported hunter-to-hunter disrespect issue had to do with shooting at game. Waterfowl and pheasant hunters talked in great length about this problem. Waterfowl hunters were upset with sky busting which scattered birds and changed a flight pattern that would have allowed for good shooting or resulted in birds staying high as they crossed firing lines. Hunters that used decoys reported that birds would begin to work their set but as they circled and began to come down, another party would begin shooting. They interpreted this as a blatant show of disrespect. Many water-fowlers felt that waterfowl hunters needed to develop the skill to accurately estimate distance of flying birds, and suggested that a test should be developed and passed to verify the skill. Without this skill, they often sky busted, not purposely trying for impossible shots but simply not having an accurate estimation of the distance to the bird.

Pheasant hunters hunting on public grounds had the problem of discriminate shooting in pursuit of flushed birds. Hunters stated that when they jumped a bird that would fly but a short distance and sit down, it was their right to follow after the bird for a second flush, but often would have a different party see the bird go down and get to it first. They also talked about being cut off by fellow hunters and explained that they would be hunting in a line, covering a particular area when another party would cross in front of them or cut in ahead and hunt out an area that they obviously would have covered themselves.

Whitetail hunters reported that large parties, who made drives as their primary hunting procedure, would drive an area they were hunting. Oftentimes drivers would pass within short distances of them. They stated there was no respect or regard granted them, as the large party drove the area, shooting at deer that were being pushed and, in the process of the drive, moved all the deer out of the area.

The third most reported concern of disrespect for fellow hunters had to do with retrieval. Both the waterfowl and pheasant hunters reported they had shot birds that came down close to other hunters and the other hunter then took the birds. We heard stories, sometimes funny, that dealt with the retrieval phenomenon. One duck hunter told how he would wear heavy boots to his firing blind to keep dry, but when the flight would start he would change to tennis shoes so he could run faster to get to the birds he had downed. Another told of watching two hunters get to a downed goose at the same time, each grabbing a wing and starting to pull until one had the bird, the other, a wing. Another told of watching a particular firing line hunter that had an excellent retriever who was constantly being sent out to get everyone's downed birds, when the dog brought back one over the limit, the warden stepped out of the grass and cited the owner.

For whitetail hunters, the problem of rights to a wounded deer or finding a dead deer while hunting was continually reported. Hunters often referred to an unwritten code that the last one to shoot an animal had the right to it. This code was questioned when a hunter, who had seriously wounded a deer, was following it, didn't hear a shot being fired and, within a short distance, found a hunter dressing out the animal and it had been tagged. The question was asked, "Should the animal be tagged or should there be a reasonable amount of time allowed for tracking and finding the animal?"

Whitetail hunters expressed, with considerable emotion, that it was upsetting to have shot an animal that had not traveled a long distance, to have not heard a shot, and to then come upon someone who had tagged it. They felt this was an act of disrespect.

Many stated they felt an animal that was seriously wounded and could easily be retrieved by the original shooter should be finished off when it passed another hunter, but reasonable time should be allowed for the original hunter to claim his/her kill. "Seriously wounded" and "reasonable time" are judgmental decisions. When the interviewers asked what constituted seriously wounded or reasonable time, there was no agreed upon definition.

Another scenario that was often related regarded the tagging of a whitetail that they had not shot, but instead found. Some hunters stated that under no circumstance would they tag an animal they had not shot. They often indicated they would dress it out if they came across a freshly killed animal, but they would not take it out of the woods. This leads to another question of ethics. Should a hunter dress out and then leave untagged deer, which is illegal in the state of Wisconsin? And a second question arises. Should dead deer be left in the woods?

Due to the various positions expressed regarding the following of wounded animals or tagging found dead whitetails, we formed small groups of whitetail hunters and asked them to discuss and recommend what the ethical response would be to different situations. The meetings got very heated as different hunters had strong feelings of what should be done. There was no final unanimous decision as to what was the most ethical response to each situation.

I conducted the meetings and felt there was a generally agreed upon position that a whitetail found that had been recently killed should be dressed and tagged by the finder after a reasonable amount of time had lapsed. They defined a reasonable time as waiting until the end of the day, or if it was cold, leaving it until the next evening. I challenged them with the legality issue of dressing out and then leaving an untagged deer. The majority stated that they would take the chance of an arrest. A minority kept to their original thought that you should leave the animal and walk away.

Regarding finishing off a wounded animal and tagging it, there was a more general agreement that if the animal was wounded, it should be finished off and left for at least two hours before being dressed out and tagged. They felt that in November the temperature in Wisconsin was normally cold enough that there was little chance of spoilage, and that two hours was a reasonable amount of time for the hunter to find the animal. If the original shooter had waited for the animal to lie down, the shot would be a signal for him to follow the animal and check out the situation. When asked about what constituted a serious wound, the definition was a wound that would cause the animal to die on its own within the next twelve hours. They felt this would take into account serious bleeding, lung damage, kidney or liver damage, or stomach puncture.

Hunters talked with a deep sense of commitment about the need of hunters to exemplify a model of hunting that assured a quick, clean kill. During the home interviews eighty-five percent of the hunters related this fact.

The Ethical Hunter Abides by Fair Chase

Ethical hunters respected game that was being hunted by adhering to the principles of fair chase. He/she did not take advantage of the animal's natural ability to survive by hunting in a way that put the animal at a disadvantage.

The late Dr. Bob Jackson, my research partner, the late Dr. Ray Anderson, then a faculty member of the Natural Resource Department, University of Wisconsin - Stevens Point, and I presented a paper at a North America Wildlife conference. The presentation was done for two purposes: 1) to assess practices that are counter-productive to the concept of fair chase; and 2) to develop an evaluation of hunting practices that put the hunter at an unfair advantage by de-emphasizing the natural ability of the animals to survive and limiting the challenge of the hunt. The following is quoted from the paper; and introduces my personal position regarding the issue of fair chase:

Hunting has changed throughout history. The needs of primitive people, the hunter and food gathered, were undoubtedly utilitarian. They were motivated to secure animals for food and fiber. Hunting was the expectation of securing food and fiber was also a necessary and important aspect of the frontier society in North America when game was plentiful and hunters few. Utilitarian hunting (Kellert, 1980) evolved in various cultures and still exists within a few societies. Today, however, hunting motivations are largely related to human recreation (recreation refers to the fact that hunting is not of absolute necessity for gathering food.) Hunting traditions, and subsequent rituals, have undergone an evolution. Professional wildlife managers have historically responded to this evolution by managing wildlife populations in a fashion that will provide the greatest number of harvested animals and by creating hunting situations that maximizes harvest opportunities. A continuously dwindling habitat base, coupled with an increasing hunter population, concentrates hunters and induces a modification of previous hunting methods so that the hunter may bag an animal. Increased hunter demands, born out of learned expectations, compel wildlife agencies to manage wild and artificial populations and hunting situations even more intensely (Borwn, 1977). In the process, some important components of the hunting experience may erode away and become lost.

In assessing the significance of the lost or distorted components, we suggest that certain management and hunting practices be evaluated by a Leopold theorem (1933). "The recreational value of a head of game is inverse to the artificiality of its origin, and hence, in a broad way to the intensity of the system of game management which produced it."

To illustrate, concentrations of deer hunters develop in some areas in densities of more than 100 per square mile with the hunter outnumbering the deer by ratios as high as four to one.

The hunter cannot practice true hunting under these circumstances, but he does adapt to the new situation by merely standing in a likely area and watching for an animal that has been moved by an unknown hunter and then shooting it, or at it when it passes. This becomes an accepted method of hunting and hunters purposely seek out areas where there are enough other hunters to "move the deer". Participation in a true hunt gives way to the development of new, more artificial practices.

Derived from the same Leopold theorem, we propose a definition of a true hunt as the opportunity to practice hunting skills under conditions in which the animal is permitted its normal behavior pattern (appropriate to the season) in its natural habitat; consequently hunting skills must include an intimate knowledge of the quarry's daily and seasonal activities and of the area being hunted. Some historical and current management practices are counter-productive to this definition and may, in fact, distort both hunting behaviors and the professional values held by some managers.

For example, wetland management plans are designed to facilitate the harvest through a pattern series of crop rotation, food growing, and re-flooding in time for the arrival of migrating ducks. Waterfowl shooters are attracted to, and become concentrated in, such baited areas. The Canada goose population in the Mississippi flyway is managed at levels far above historic populations to meet the expectation of today's goose shooters. Disease threatens these unnatural concentrated populations and considerable research management efforts have gone into finding methods of dispensing the population over a wider area to provide shooting for more hunters and to minimize the disease potential.

Shooters harvest geese from permanently positioned blinds on public lands after receiving cursory instructions from agency wildlife managers at the site. Geese are baited to "landing strips" of freshly sprouted winter wheat or rye for shooting on public lands. The four-inch new growth is timed to coincide with the peak of goose migration. Hunters concentrate in long firing lines on the periphery of refuges, adorned with tennis shoes to facilitate the foot races to downed birds. They consider it a successful hunt if they burn up several boxes of shells while shooting at high flying geese, and highly successful if they are fortunate enough to be the first to get a downed bird. The art of actually hunting geese by observing feeding patterns, blind positioning, and decoying is rare and becoming rarer.

Doves are baited into shooting positions on public lands by cultivating areas of sorghum in strategic locations. The shooting season is set to open after the doves have become conditioned to the undisturbed feeding situation. Shooters are permitted (encouraged?) to literally surround the field and, in doing so, jeopardize each other's safety with concentrated shooting. Personnel from local television stations shield their camera lenses from the raining shots as they record the event to provide the general public a first-hand account of modern hunting. This dove management was considered to be so successful by one wildlife manager that he seriously considered applying the same practice to prairie chickens. Success in these cases is measured in numbers of birds harvested per shooter.

Forest trails and roads are seeded to white clover to bait ruffed grouse into a position where they are more accessible to shooters; woody vegetation is cut back along the edges of roads to provide better shooting. The grouse do not need the clover in the fall, a time of the year when a variety of natural foods are super abundant, but this practice has become synonymous with ruffed grouse management. The number of grouse harvested per mile of road driven has become the measure of success, and hunting with a motorized vehicle has become an accepted method. For many, it is the only method.

New equipment and gadgetry made hunting more comfortable and the game more accessible with less physical effort. Pick-up trucks, airboats, snowmobiles, and ATVs become standard equipment for hunting many species. Equipment that provides the hunter with undue advantage over the wild one is often accepted or ignored by wildlife managers who judge the success of a season in terms of the total harvest and high hunter success ratios. New hunters who find these practices appealing, are initiated under the system and practice grows geometrically, much more rapidly than one generation at a time as in the past. New ethics evolve concomitantly with the change in methods and equipment.

As the demand for game increases, and the supply becomes scarcer, game managers search for methods that will further increase the supply to meet the demand.

These managers then adopt and justify artificial techniques to put something in the game bag to satisfy the hunter who has now become merely a shooter. These managers take the ultimate step and resurrect the practice of rearing animals in captivity to ensure maximum production and then release them before the gun under quasi-natural conditions, e.g. the pheasant stocking programs.

Methods of shooting that develop around the maintenance stocking practice include following the stocking trucks to the release site and shooting the birds as they are released, although some agencies attempt to insulate their hunting clientele by secretly stocking the birds at an unobtrusive time. Motivation to shoot a "wild" animal are fulfilled, the methods become traditional, and the practice becomes a ritual to be taught to new hunters and passed on to succeeding generations. These recreationlists sincerely believe they are hunting. They naively practice that which was considered to be unethical and unsportsmanlike only a short time ago simply because they know of no other way.

Our challenge, as hunters, is to teach ourselves and others that there is another way, to help all of us understand that hunting is not gadgetry, specialized equipment, baiting, or pursuing animals that were hatched or born in captivity and released. Instead, hunting is the pursuit of animals that have the advantage of natural movement in a natural environment. Violation and absence of fair chase, both factors that rob hunters and hunting of dignity, can only be eliminated by each hunter taking the time to examine and understand the consequences of the acts and then, to make a connection on a personal level to not violate and to respect fair chase.

Our research verified that hunters are different, with different inductions into hunting, different levels of hunting skills, and different levels of intensity, all which impact upon the concept of fair chase. The success of the hunt was more complicated than any one of the following by itself: numbers harvested, days infield, hunter density, game abundance or scarcity, weather during the actual hunting season, safety, behavior of other hunters, or availability of hunting land.

Game managers are caught in the bind of mid-management. They are required to develop overall management plans that meet the various needs of the hunter, the consumer, and, at the same time, meet DNR department needs for license sales revenues. License sale promotions rely upon the idea that managers should put a whitetail behind every tree and a bird behind every bush. The DNR promotions to draw hunters for license revenue publicizes the idea that game was abundant. The hunter therefore anticipates a high probability of harvesting game under low hunter density and catch twenty-two becomes a reality.

When discussing the issue of fair chase with game managers, they emphasized that game management will become more diverse into the twenty-first century, as it will continue to emphasize and perfect the concept of ecosystem management. Management areas that were traditionally defined by roads, waterways, and fences are redefined by watershed areas. The redefining of the borders then incorporates more diverse landform areas, watershed, public and private land ownership, and the need to manage for more diverse human, wildlife, and landscape needs.

Management will continue to take on a more developed team approach utilizing the expertise of lay people representing the vast needs of all who want to experience the land. Planning will rely upon the expertise of DNR fishery, forestry, and wildlife professionals and the utilization of university and private enterprise personnel. Decisions for development of public properties will take on a broader, more careful, and deliberate decision-making process. Land that was once primarily managed for hunting will be scrutinized and have more management objectives added.

The lands carrying capacity for deer and game bird populations, length and time of seasons, harvest quotas, hunting methods, the landscape itself, and utilization by individuals and groups that are not necessarily hunters will become a significant part of the process in deciding how land will be managed. It is important that hunters understand this process and articulate their wants to provide direction and momentum to wildlife managers to ensure that their wants become an integral part of ecosystem management.

Fair chase is how hunted game ultimately receives the worth and recognition it deserves and needs to become one of the primary objectives of every wildlife management plan. Sixty-five percent of the hunters we interviewed stated that fair chase and ethical hunting are synonymous. They expressed the opinion that birds or animal harvested by elimination of fair chase caused the kill to be of less status, resulting in less respect for the animal and greater the chance for violation of its rights.

Equipment that interrupts the natural movement of deer forces animals to move in prescribed ways so they can be shot by positioned hunters or places hunters in areas that are reasonably obtainable by walking, all devalue the hunt. Hunters voiced strong negative comments concerning their use.

Gadgetry and equipment can become the primary means by which a hunter rates hunter satisfaction. Do we really need to have strings or radar beams set across deer runways that can be set off by an animal that is moving through and record when it happened? Do we really need baiting machines that are set to timers to dispel the bait at specific times to condition whitetails to be there when we want them? Do we really need ATVs that deliver us to the spot of the hunt, instead of us walking to the hunting area?

During interview sessions we used tree stands as a beginning point for discussion relating to equipment that could put the hunter at an advantage and the animal at a disadvantage. We got two different perspectives from bow and firearm hunters. The bow hunter saw the tree stand as a necessity. It addressed the issue of a quick, clean kill. They stated it would put them in the whitetail's natural world. After they studied the land and understood the animal's movement they were able to place the stand for a killing shot. The placement of the tree stand and their ability to accurately shoot the bow were the two prime factors in successful harvest. Placement of the shot within a close distance had to be managed and the tree stand was a must.

For gun hunters, the discussion was not so cut and dry as numerous hunters felt the practice needed to be evaluated. Gun hunters had three prime perspectives that were brought into the discussion. One of the perspectives dealt with the issue of a clean, quick kill. The second one dealt with type of stand. The third pertained to the hunter who could only hunt for a short period of time and did not have the opportunity for scouting prior to the opening of the season. This hunter was put at a significant disadvantage as the place and placement of a stand required pre-season scouting as well as time to put the stand in place. There was no consensus of thought, but there were strong opinions expressed.

There was an agreement that the tree stand increased the probability of a quick, clean kill and increased the safety factor of knowing what was behind the line of fire as the shooting angle caused the bullet to stop quickly. Even though there was agreement on these two points, many felt it degraded the hunt and should not be allowed. Hunters talked about the bow hunters' tree stand and the gun hunters' tree house and how they were usually two very different structures. Tree houses with windows to shoot from, heaters to keep warm and cook on, and in some, cots to take a rest, were thought to degrade the natural environment and devalue the concept of a hunt. They stated that the hunt should take place in the natural environment and be part of the natural environment, which dictates that the elements of weather, wind, snow, rain, or heat needed to be tolerated and controlled by appropriate dress.

The tree stand issue was then followed by questions about baiting. The majority of hunters stated the most blatant abuse of fair chase was baiting. Whitetails operate under the same principles as all other animals. They take the path of least resistance, so when bait was provided as part of their food supply, they came. They established bedding and movement patterns based upon where the baited food source was placed and predictability became easily accomplished. Whitetails came to the feed lot first, so they often appeared before dark, took their quota of the bait, then moved to natural browse after dark, which caused them to become easy targets at the baiting site. Bait was placed in their natural surroundings so it unobtrusively became a part of what would appear to be a natural food source, taking advantage of the animals' normal curiosity and fear of unnatural surroundings.

The artificial stage was set when bait appeared. It changed the natural movement of the whitetail by creating a feeding center causing the animal to stay within the vicinity of the bait. When one person baited, it often caused others to bait also. This, in turn, acts like a magnet to draw animals from all around.

Fred, my bow hunting partner, and I went up to Northern Wisconsin during a bow season for a three day hunt. We set up stands in an area I was familiar with and knew the movement and feeding patterns of the deer. The area had excellent natural browse, fields of clover or winter rye, small islands in a large spruce swamp where the deer bed, and poplar ridges with major crossings.

We set up our stands in early afternoon, then left to return the next morning for the hunt and during the night about two inches of new snow fell. We got into our stands before daylight and when light came, there were no whitetails, nor were there any signs that any had moved through. We spent the day without seeing a single whitetail, returned the second day, no sign again, not even one track in the snow.

At mid-morning on the second day, we took a walk onto private land, which I had permission to walk on but not hunt. About two hundred yards from where we had been hunting we started to find signs. Within another one hundred yards we found trails and then consistently jumped bedding whitetails. We followed one of the main trails that paralleled the edge of a swamp and came upon a large bait pile, a combination of corn, potatoes and rutabagas. The illegal bait pile had a tree stand over it.

Animals that are susceptible to baiting are also used by business and private individuals for either economic or personal enjoyment. In either case, the process of taking a wild animal and partially domesticating it by systematic feeding sets the stage for it to lose most of its natural survival instincts.

Whitetails being fed in people's yards, often on the perimeter of an urban settlement, have created a major problem. These people entice animals into an environment where they loose many of their natural survival instincts and become susceptible to car kills. They stay close to their food source and begin the process of reproduction in urban areas. Within five years, a breeding doe has produced approximately sixty-one more of its kind, and then the problem of what to do with them as they browse away lawn, flowers, and shrubbery becomes an issue. The act of baiting results in major problems for people and the animal.

Our interviewers asked hunters that baited if they felt it was ethical. The majority said they saw no ethical implications. When asked about fair chase, they either avoided the question or admitted that fair chase was not something they thought about. Many attempted to justify baiting on the grounds that they were doing the deer a favor by feeding them year round and were assisting the survival rate by providing food during the winter. When asked if they felt challenged when shooting deer over bait, they seldom answered the question.

The rationale of feeding deer to maintain the herd does not stand up. Seldom are winters severe enough to cause major winter-kills, and when they are, the artificial feeding of malnourished deer has minimal results. Studies indicate it might save about an additional three percent of the herd that would have died had feeding not been instrumented. Having well nourished deer going into winter from good summer feeding patterns is the key to a healthy deer herd.

Baiting psychologically puts into place the process of expecting to get the game. Financial investment puts a high premium on the head, and, as Leopold stated, "a head of game is inverse to the artificiality of its origin." The concept of the hunt becomes lost and the animal becomes equated to the right of kill because of financial investment. A whitetail taken under this mindset has minimal value as a prized accomplishment. It does not compare to taking the animal as a result of a natural hunt.

During the summer of 2000, I interviewed nineteen bow

hunters one-on-one who had only hunted over bait. I was attempting to gather information pertaining to their motivation and satisfaction. The first set of questions was directed toward their motivation. The "why do you hunt" question had very homogenous responses as they centered on four perspectives: we see a lot of deer, find enjoyment in watching them interact, enjoy being outside during the changing of the season, and bait sets up a situation for a good, close killing shot.

The second set of questions was directed towards preparation for the upcoming hunting season. Their responses focused on bow preparation and maintenance, practice shooting, and pre-season baiting.

The third probe explored their overall plan for harvesting a whitetail. Each individual response was closely related. They did little to no pre-season scouting. They used the same stands year after year, so there was no need to find natural routes of deer movement. The deer came to the bait. Two of the nineteen related that they were after trophies, and they did the majority of hunting during December, capitalizing on deer movement during the warmest part of the day. The other seventeen said they would take the first good buck during the early part of the season, and would then switch to harvesting a doe. When asked what constituted a good buck, the most common answer was, "not a spike or fork horn."

The last question asked was, "What was most challenging about your hunting experience?" The most common response was the delivery of a well-placed shot. The response from two of the hunters was actually hard for me to believe. I could not believe what I was hearing. They said it was the proper placement of the bait. Each went into great detail of how they placed the bait to cause the animal to have to reach down and stretch its neck, opening up a broadside lung shot. Each used fallen trees and uneven terrain to force a prescribed entry to the bait. It went on and on.

When I reviewed the responses, in terms of motivation and satisfaction, they closely paralleled data from the study that reflected developmental stages one or two.

Baiting violated multiple ethical standards. The most blatant being fair chase. It also placed the herd in jeopardy by contributing to the transmission of disease by concentrated feeding. It created conflict between hunters over deer distribution and hindered hunters from developing to a level where the challenge and satisfaction of the harvest of a whitetail resulted due to knowledge of the animal's habits and habitat. It caused the hunter to miss the experience and reward of hunting for a trophy and precludes the experience of the hunt itself being the ultimate satisfaction. I strongly believe the practice of baiting needs to be stopped.

Fair chase is how the hunter gains respect for the game he/she is hunting. When game is harvested by less than fair chase standards, the prized accomplishment is diminished.

The ethical hunter, the dedicated sportsman or sportswoman, where hunting is an integral part of their quality world, abides by and advocates for legislated laws which regulate the hunt. They honor the land, respect the landowners, the non-hunter, fellow hunters and respect fair chase. They are the true hunters, and deserve the title and privilege of being called "hunter".

CHAPTER 4

VIOLATORS

A Blog on Our Sport

What would you do if a member of your hunting party violated the law or if you saw another hunter violate the law?

Violations happened as the "slob" hunted and displayed unethical behavior. This reinforced a negative image of hunters. During twenty-two years of research, we had the opportunity to talk with numerous hunters who admitted to violating. We had trained observers who recorded violator behavior during the time of their hunt and had landowners record violator behavior during a nine-day deer firearm season. Hunters who participated in one-on-one interviews and those that were involved in small group discussions were also asked questions and to share perceptions about violators.

We designed four studies to provide specific data relating to violators and issues surrounding violating. The first study pertained to duck hunters and data was collected by direct observation of hunts. The second study focused on firearm deer hunters. We were not able to design an observable aspect for the study. Therefore, data was collected through in-field interviews completed at the end of hunts and then during two hour in-home, follow up interviews. The third study had landowners record hunter behaviors on their property during a nine day firearm, deer season. The forth study focused on habitual violators and was completed through one-on-one interviews.

Valuable data and insight regarding violator behavior was also gathered during the in-depth home interviews. Over two thousand hunters shared their insights. Hunters also participated in small focus discussions where they analyzed violators and issues pertaining to violating.

Duck Hunter Study

The duck hunter study provided us with the most reliable data pertaining to violator behavior. Data was collected through direct observation of the hunter as he/she hunted.

Retired game wardens trained university students from UW La Crosse and UW Stevens Point as observers. The wardens trained them with observational techniques and knowledge of the law. Bob Jackson and I trained them in recording procedure and duck identification. When observers demonstrated they knew legal and ethical aspects of duck hunting, and were proficient in recording procedures as well as duck identification, they went into marshes with the wardens to observe and recorded a hunt. When both the student and warden observation and recordings matched, the student was certified to complete individual observations independently.

Wardens established spy blind positions. Observers would then position themselves prior to a hunter's arrival, and then record that hunter's behavior as the hunt progressed. We observed six hundred fifty hunts over a three-year period.

Hunter behavior was recorded on a standardized form. Observers recorded shooting opportunities, birds hit or missed, birds retrieved, law-abiding or violating behavior, ethical or unethical behavior, hunting style, and, at the end of the hunt was given a rating on degree of hunting expertise.

When the hunter began preparation for the completion of the hunt, the observer attempted to reach the landing prior to the hunter's return. When the hunter returned to the landing, the observer asked if he/she would agree to a short interview regarding their just completed hunt. The hunter was not told that he/she had been observed. If the hunter asked if he had been observed, he was honestly answered, and his hunt was then culled from the study. Hunters were very cooperative and seldom turned down the interview. The observer/interviewer asked questions that would be correlated with the observation of the completed hunt. Questions about behavior of other hunters, degree of shooting accuracy and retrieval of hit birds, number of shots taken, level of satisfaction, and would they be willing to participate in a follow-up post season interview. The post-season interviewers did not have knowledge of the recorded responses to assure no bias when conducting the follow up interview.

Because the hunt had been observed, we knew who had committed illegal as well as ethical violations, and out of a final pool of five hundred seventy-nine observations, we completed four hundred forty-two post season in-home interviews. Twenty-one percent of the hunters had committed a legal violation.

We listened to our in depth interviewers, reviewed the data from the post season and follow up interviews and compared the information to what we knew from the observed hunts. We then classified the violators into four different categories: the non-avoidable or non-intentional violators, those ignorant of the law, the opportunistic, and the habitual or professional violator.

The non-avoidable or non-intentional category pertained to violations that were difficult to keep from happening. I had a situation happen that fits into this category. In Wisconsin, we had a four duck limit and it specified numbers of particular birds. I was jump shooting and had shot a pair of wood ducks then decided I would attempt to limit out with a pair of greenheads.

I was hunting in a marsh and knew where there was a strong possibility of some mallards. The particular waterway I was headed for could be observed from a point about one hundred yards away and I could see five mallards, two of them being greenheads. I crawled up to a pond, got in position, and stood up. The birds jumped and I concentrated to find the drakes, saw one, pulled and saw it crumple, pulled on the other and down it went.

I knew the second bird was hit hard, so I went to where I had shot the first bird and found a dead hen and drake. When I shot I had no idea there was a hen that close to the drake. I was now one over the limit and had to make a decision whether or not to discard one duck. It was not an easy choice, and it entered my mind that I could dress all three, leave one and pick it up the next day and count it as part of that day's limit. I did have a debate with myself, as drawing the bird was disregarding the law, so I left it. I picked it up the next day and dressed it because the nights were getting cold, and leaving it overnight did not harm the bird.

These are the dilemmas of a hunter who had to rely upon his/her own sense of fair play: there are no umpires or referees, only one's own judgment and conscience. If I had been observed by one of the trained observers, the incident would have been rated as a violation if I had drawn the bird or continued to hunt, since an over the limit rule would have been applied. The observers documented that seldom was an over limit duck left, but instead resulted as an intentional violation as the hunter took the bird and yet continued to hunt.

It is illegal to break down muskrat houses. There were three times during the observed hunts that muskrat houses were either run upon by a boat or stepped on during retrieval of a bird. In all three instances, the observer recorded that the houses were difficult to detect and therefore, these hunters did not realize the rat house was present. We recorded the violation as non-intentional.

Violations that occurred due to ignorance of the law happened when the hunter had not taken the time to become informed. The excuse that there were so many regulations that the hunter could not keep track of them was not acceptable. We heard this story often in the post-season interview and it usually came from one who had violated. We seldom heard it from the seventy-nine percent that obeyed the regulations. It was the hunter's responsibility to become aware of the law, and if there was confusion, it was his/her responsibility to call the local warden and get clarification. We had no way to determine the actual number of violations due to ignorance.

The opportunistic violator was one who planned and acted upon his plan. "I will violate because I believe I have a small probability of getting caught. Limits do not apply to me. "How I get the game doesn't matter. I will hunt where and when I please. I have no responsibility to the game or to fellow hunters." We called this kind of hunter the "slob". He is a poacher who leaves home with larceny in his heart and the tools to accomplish it.

The opportunistic duck hunter violator knew how to create shooting possibilities and took more chances to capitalize on those possibilities. Simply put, they knew what they were doing, they knew where to go, they took more chances, and they took a larger portion of game than the non-violator. A profile of the opportunistic violator looked like the following. Opportunity began with birds being available to the gun. The violator had twice as many shooting opportunities as the non-violator. They knew where to hunt and where to be situated. Violators were observed shooting an average of 11.7 rounds per hunting trip in contrast to 5.4 shots taken by non-violators. Along with the increased opportunity to shoot, they more often shot at unethical distances. Twenty-five percent of the non-violators failed to fire a single shot during the observed hunt.

Opportunistic violators achieved a greater daily and seasonal bag limit. Non-violators averaged .53 ducks per hunt and failed to bag any ducks seventy-three percent of the time. Violators averaged .91 ducks per hunt and failed to bag any ducks fifty-five percent of the time. During the post-season interview, hunters were asked to estimate the number of ducks they shot during the season. Violators reported shooting eighteen ducks, non-violators estimated fourteen. For hunters who claimed to have shot more than twenty ducks per season, the violation ratio was twenty-eight percent.

The violator was more intensely involved in duck hunting than the non-violator. They had invested a greater amount of time, energy, and money into their hunting. Fifty-eight percent of the violators shot trap or skeet as opposed to forty-four percent of the non-violators. Thirty-seven percent of the violators used a dog as compared to twenty-one percent of the non-violators. A significantly larger percent of the violators used a duck call, had a camouflaged boat, read technical hunting magazines to increase their hunting skills, and prepared a blind before the season began.

One popular scapegoat of Wisconsin hunters was the non-local hunter who traveled a distance on weekends to prime waterfowl habitat and usually came from an urban area. They were projected as the uninformed, unsafe, non-ethical hunter. The data did not support this assertion. The rate of violations for non-local hunters was fifteen percent as compared to twenty-five percent to those who lived twenty-five miles or less from where the hunt was observed.

Violations were also analyzed by day of the week. The highest day of violations, thirty-six percent, was on Friday. Further analysis of the Friday hunter indicated that they were likely to be local hunters. The post season interviewers reported numerous reports of local hunters who said they tried to get Fridays off from work so they could get a jump on the expected influx of non-locals who would be arriving for the weekend hunt. The average age for violators was twenty-eight as compared to thirty-four for non-violators. The average number of years hunting by violators was twelve as compared to seventeen for non-violators. Data indicated that the rate of violation dropped considerably for those who had hunted more than twenty years.

Thirty-one percent of the violators were judged to have displayed unethical behavior during the hunt. These behaviors were principally shooting at ducks out of range and crowding other hunters. Positive behaviors were also noted by the observer. Thirty-nine percent of the violators were observed displaying good sportsmanship as compared to sixty-one percent of the non-violators.

During the interview that immediately followed the hunt, hunters were asked to rate their satisfaction for that day's hunt on a four point scale: excellent, good, fair, or poor. Violators were significantly more likely to report a higher satisfaction with the day's hunt. Fifty-one percent of the violators reported the day as either excellent or good. When asked what was most satisfying with a hunt, violators indicated that bag, shooting opportunities, and competition with other hunters were the basis for their satisfaction. Non-violators, in contrast, reported that companionship, seeing game, and an opportunity to observe nature were the most satisfying ingredients of their hunt.

Hunters were asked during the post season interview how ethics could be improved. Violators were more likely to indicate that hunting ethics could not be changed. Non-violators were more optimistic and suggested that laws and peer group pressure could improve hunters' ethics.

Violations were primarily the result of opportunistic behavior. The violator has the ability to know where to hunt to increase the probability of increased bag, takes more chances of bagging by taking more shots, thus killing more birds, invests more time, energy and money, more than likely lives within twenty-five miles of the infraction, will take shots that are beyond reasonable shotgun range, will be less tolerant of fellow hunters by crowding them, will be more satisfied with the hunt (satisfaction will correlate with birds killed, shooting opportunities, and competition with other hunters), and see little likelihood of improving hunter ethics.

Whitetail Hunter Study

We were not able to design a study of whitetail hunters where we could train students to observe and record hunter behavior as we did in the duck hunter study. We had to rely upon in-field and post season interviews and data collected from landowners to ascertain types and degrees of violation. I tried, on three attempts, to do in-field observations of whitetail hunters. The first time, I attempted to shadow a hunter as he moved through the woods on a silent stalking hunt. I kept losing him. When I would find him, oftentimes I'd be right next to him. I was carrying a rifle and posing as a hunter, yet had pen and paper for recording, and I imagine a scurried look on my face as I almost bumped into him. He looked at me with disgust and his annoyance increased with each encounter.

The next attempt was done by my trying to conceal myself on a hilltop in an area of scrub oak trees, thinking I could watch with glasses. It was on a cold day in November, and even colder on the top of a hill with the wind blowing. When a hunter would appear, I would get the recording sheet out and, by the time I got my fingers warmed up so I could record, the hunter was gone.

On my third attempt, I again tried to shadow a moving

hunter, but this time chose an area that was semi-open and hilly, with a scattering of scrub oak. The oaks hold their leaves late in the fall so they made for a significant amount of cover. I stayed after him for about three hours, thinking he had not seen me, then he went over a small hill, and I lost him. I slowly made my way over the hill, but he was nowhere in sight. I was frantically looking for him, and, as I walked over a second hill, I walked into the barrel of a 30.06 pointed at me with an upset hunter who asked, "What in the hell are you doing?" Bob and I decided that we scrap the direct observation data collection and use in-field observations, home interviews and landowner observation for data on violations of whitetail hunters.

We interviewed about eleven hundred whitetail hunters in the field, immediately following their hunt by having trained interviewers in the woods or waiting at their parked vehicles.

Of the eleven hundred field interviews, we followed up with two hundred eight home interviews, each lasting approximately two hours, where we were able to discuss pertinent issues regarding gun-hunting whitetails and ask about violations. The hunters were asked to rate the seriousness of a number of problem areas that pertained to gun hunting whitetails. They rated poaching or the shooting illegal deer during the hunting season and leaving them in the woods as the two most significant problem areas. Forty-four percent of those interviewed said they had found or saw dead whitetails left in the woods during their hunting experience. Thirty-seven percent said they had noted violations during the last hunting season.

In Wisconsin it is illegal to have a loaded or uncased gun in a vehicle, or to shoot from a public road. These were consistently reported violations. Thirty-three percent of the hunters stated they heard shooting before or after legal shooting hours. Thirty-three percent said they personally knew of an individual who shot a deer out of season during the past year. Fourteen percent admitted that they had violated.

We asked the hunters to tell us what factors might cause hunters to violate. They stated self-ownership of the land as the highest, low probability of getting caught as second and hunting late in the season as third.

One hundred six landowners kept a log that recorded what they observed regarding hunter behavior on their land during a nine-day deer firearm hunting season. It is illegal, in Wisconsin, to hunt on private property without permission. Fifty-eight percent of the landowners recorded hunters on their land without permission. Forty-seven percent recorded violations that did not pertain to hunting without permission. The following, in order of most observed to least observed were: road hunting, shooting off public roads, shooting just before and after hours, and shooting during the night.

What can be done to curtail legal and ethical violations is a relatively simple matter. When young hunters finish their hunter education classes, they have been introduced to a model of legal and ethical hunting. They do not graduate from their classes as potential violators; it is just the opposite. If they become violators, it will be due to their hunting partner or peer group. We who hunt need to present the young hunter with an enthusiasm for hunting and a model of hunting that does not and will not tolerate violating.

Violators are a problem within our ranks that can be curtailed by us. We need to set a personal philosophy that, as individual hunters, we will not violate. We will not tolerate those that violate. We will work cooperatively with local wardens and report all violators. Bag limits, hunting methods, firearm regulations, and seasons are designed to ensure a balance of harvest with reproductive cycles. We all must work together if we are going to be able to continue the American hunting tradition.

To have young hunters become ethical and legal hunters requires a process that is three-tiered. The first tier is in place. We have young hunters who enter our ranks possessing the right hunter attitudes and beginning knowledge. The state hunter education programs do just that. Bob and I were privileged to have the opportunity to meet and work with professional hunter education specialists in many parts of the country. They were dedicated state employees who are skilled in sound educational practices and organizational strategies as they coordinated the volunteers who provided the classes. The volunteer instructors projected an example of an exemplary hunter who demonstrated high legal and ethical standards, maintained and built strong hunter traditions, demonstrated sound teaching strategies, and were dedicated to youth.

The second tier is built by experienced hunters. Experienced hunters take the young hunter from the hunter education classroom into the field to develop their hunting skills. They must be provided with an ethical model of hunting. Who the young hunter begins his/her hunting experience with will be the primary influence on his/her future hunting attitudes and behaviors.

The third tier requires hunters to take personal responsibility to define their own ethical and legal standards and be willing to monitor the behavior of other hunters. The continual involvement of hunter to hunter by promoting high hunting standards is the key to ensure exemplary hunter behavior.

I started my lifelong pursuit of whitetails when I was ten years old. My dad took me with him for two years, and, at twelve, I started to hunt with my dad as his partner. During those beginning years, I was his focus. He talked to me, showed me, at times tested me by having me stay on a stand or make a short drive to him. He was always patient, always ready to listen. He was a buck hunter. He started to hunt before the time of variable quotas and party permits that harvested antlerless deer. He did not change in the fifties and sixties, when the game manager specialist entered the scene with herd management strategies that included the harvest of antler-less deer. He still hunted bucks only. He was a hard hunter, from daylight to dark, an honest hunter, who knew the land, honored the animal, and abided by the law. I was with the right model, and when he and I hunted together, I abided by the law.

Things changed for me in my late teens and early twenties. When I hunted with a party that accepted violations, I violated. I am ashamed of what I did. I knew better, but I had identified myself to others and to me personally as a hunter, and part of that identity was to prove that I could get game. Whitetails and ducks became numbers, the higher the number, the more I proved my self-proclaimed identity. It can become a vicious cycle, which then becomes part of who you are, and eventually, limits and seasons have no meaning.

Why did I change? I would never violate when my son, Dan, was hunting with me. My Dad did not violate, and I wanted Dan to admire me as I did my dad. It was the beginning of change. Hunting and abiding by the law was actually more rewarding than breaking it and having to become a dishonest sneak. It was also during that time that I met Bob Jackson.

He was then Psychology Department Chair at the University of Wisconsin-La Crosse and hired me as an instructor in that department. Our mutually deep interest in hunting was quickly discovered, and he invited me to go with him on a duck hunt. As we got ready to go into the marsh for the first time, he told me he was a hunter who abided by strict ethical and legal standards and would turn anyone in who he saw breaking the law. He then said, "And that would include you." I knew where he stood and where I stood, and, at that moment he had my deepest respect.

We spent many, many days over the years together in the marsh, in the pheasant lands of Iowa, on the geese flyways by the Horicon Marsh, in the bottom lands and pastures where grouse lived, on the brook trout streams of south central Wisconsin, and I would never break the law when I was with him. He knew how to hunt, how to shoot, how to pursue, and how to totally enjoy the day. I again learned how totally enjoyable the hunt was when violating was not tolerated.

I now hunt with two different partners or alone. Both of my partners do not violate, and neither do I. Oscar and I have opened forty-eight consecutive gun whitetail seasons and at least forty duck seasons. Fred is my other hunting partner. We try to have at least one pheasant hunt together in either Iowa or the Dakotas, spend time fishing the boundary waters of Canada, and enjoy the Wisconsin bow season as hunting partners, and pursue the ruffed grouse.

My grandsons, Zack and Wildon, have both finished their hunter education class and join Oscar and me during the whitetail season. They will be true hunters, ethical and legal hunters; I will help them.

The Habitual, Professional Violator

I hesitate to write about the habitual or professional violator, first because I wished they did not exist, and secondly, I personally know little about them. We took a special interest and tried to find out what would motivate anyone to have this level of disregard for the law, for hunting, and for one's own sense of worth. Bob contacted the Wisconsin Department of Natural Resources to ascertain names of habitual violators. He was provided with names of ten individuals who had arrest records of multiple convictions for violations.

I contacted each of them and explained that we were doing research on the behavior, motivation, and ethics of hunters. We were interested in talking with individuals who had been convicted of hunting violations, assured them of absolute confidentiality so they need not be concerned that anyone would know their identity and asked if they would be willing to meet me at a place of their choice and talk.

Two of the ten agreed to meet. The other eight expressed a strong dislike for the Department of Natural Resources, the court system, and people like me, and let it be known that they wanted no part of what we were doing.

Interviews with two individuals does not provide enough data to make judgments and present a case as to what causes a person to become a habitual violator. A second factor to keep in mind was they had both been proven to be dishonest. So when interviewing them, there was a possibility that they might not tell the truth. I had no way to verify the information they were providing, as they were assured of confidentiality. This meant that I would not attempt to find additional information regarding them.

Both men said they had stopped violating. When asked why, one reported that he did all his violating with two other men and they had relocated due to their work. When he lost his partners, he stopped. The second said he had three sons and all of them wanted to hunt, he did not want them to be violators.

Both men appeared to have gained respect both at work and in their community, one being self-employed, and the other employed in the health profession. They participated in community events, and each were members of local service organizations. They were an integral part of their families, enjoyed travel, family gatherings, and activities.

Neither of them talked about their specific conviction record. They volunteered that they had been cited but appeared to be nonchalant regarding the conviction. They did not indicate that what they did was wrong nor did they indicate any wrong treatment at the time of the citation or during court proceedings.

I asked them why they had violated. There were some similarities as well as differences. Neither of them violated alone. One had two partners, the other had one. Both talked at length about the close relationships of the partners, of how they perfected roles or jobs, how they depended on each other, how they perfected equipment, and the success and excitement they experienced as they took game.

The threesome was involved in illegal killing of whitetails. He said they did their entire killing along a specific stretch of secondary blacktop road. They would meet at the home of the person I was interviewing, during October and early November. After dark they enacted their plan.

Whitetails fed along an open roadway, and were all shot

from the car. Each of the three had a specific job during the shooting: driver, spotlighter, and shooter. Once the deer was shot it was left, and a marker was dropped along the edge of the road to designate points for pick-up later that night. The brake lights of the car were wired so a control switch could be used to keep the lights from coming on to minimize concern of other drivers or give away their position.

They would continue on their course until they had killed four or five deer. They would then backtrack and pick up the deer. They had a station wagon designed with a large floor box and no interior lights. The driver would stop at a marker; the spot lighter and shooter would get out of the car and get the deer. The driver would open the tailgate and the deer would be thrown in the box. They would continue to the next marker until all the deer were loaded. The deer were taken to a farm that had a butcher house, dressed, skinned, and sold. I asked how many deer they would kill each fall and he said, "About a hundred."

The second individual I interviewed talked in length about he and his partner's venture into illegal spear fishing. He was extremely expressive and proud of the special equipment they had designed. The lights were designed to be kept under water all the time to keep them from being spotted while on the lake. They were made so the driver of the boat could manipulate them to shine underwater areas from his position in the back of the boat. They were designed from spotlights used by plugging into cigarette lighters of cars, thus enabling one person to drive the boat and be the spotter.

The person I interviewed was the driver/spotter. They had designed a spear from stainless steel that was extendable by snapping lengths together, which took only a half turn to complete. This allowed them to quickly adapt for depth as well as being able to break the spear down and drop it overboard if they thought they were going to be checked by a warden. He said they stared their spearing season during the spring walleye spawn and continued through the summer taking walleyes, northern, and muskies. They would start their night run around eleven, as most of the people living on or near the lake would be in bed.

They tried to pick lakes or rivers where there was a bridge or road close to the water's edge. They put the speared fish in gunnysacks to be dropped off at a designated spot. They would drop a gunny sack off at one of the drop off sites, then drive around with their car and pick them up just before daylight. I asked what they did with the fish and was told they gave most of them away.

From the substance of the two interviews, it appeared that the motivation to violate centered around the challenge to develop specialized equipment, the comradeship that developed between the individuals, the greed that is expressed by the number of illegal takes, and no real sense or need for responsibility to game laws or to people who enjoy the world of hunting and fishing.

What can be done about decreasing violations? Increased fines and loss of hunting privileges have a positive effect on stopping some violators. During the interviews a significant number of hunters said that violating wasn't worth the fine. The fine was too high, confiscation of gun and vehicle along with the loss of hunting privilege wasn't worth it. The violator's name with the violation published in newspapers brought embarrassment to the individual. Certainly, the fear of getting caught, paying the fines, financial losses, and publicity of the act the individual perpetrated have made major impacts on reducing violations.

Violations are an enormous blemish to hunting. We can eliminate most of them within our ranks. We start by making a personal commitment to hunting by studying the laws and demonstrating high personal ethical standards. We tell other hunters that we do not violate, and we will not accept it as part of the hunting experience of others. We cooperate with the wardens and let them know that we will report individuals that we see violating. We need to develop a plan of reporting by having phone numbers, times to call, and documentation that can be gathered which might be useful during warden investigations.

All hunters have responsibility to themselves and their fellow hunters to follow the law. Hunting is a self-motivated, self-chosen act. There are very few people who continue to hunt because they have to. We hunt because it is an expression of who we are and what we believe. When violating, hunters disrespect themselves, display selfishness and disregard for others (hunters and non-hunters alike) and clearly disrespect the animals that they pursue.

CHAPTER 5
WHY DO YOU HUNT?

Satisfaction, it's what keeps us coming back!

Rate your greatest to least satisfaction as a hunter. Rank your greatest satisfaction with a one, least satisfaction with a ten. See how you compare to 3,500 other hunters.

Competition

Escape and solitude

Nature appreciation

Development and utilization of hunting skills

Companionship

Use of specialized quipment (dogs, guns, decoys, electronics)

Harvesting game as a food supply

Development of outdoor skills (other than hunting)

Exercise

Testing of outdoor skills (other than hunting)

What was it that caused us to get out of a warm bed at four in the morning and go into a hostile environment of snow, rain, wind, cold, and oftentimes a combination of all four? To spend the day in a tree, walk in the woods, sit in a duck blind, walk all day in grass and muck up to our hips in a pair of waders? My wife, Carole, says it hinges on insanity, yet she knows that the force that draws us to the woods and marshes are strong and real.

To determine what hunters perceived as most satisfying about their pursuit of hunting, they rated satisfaction scales, answered open-ended questions during pre-season interviews, granted interviews immediately after a hunt was completed, participated in post-season one-on-one interviews, and as members of small focus groups.

During pre-season interviews, hunters answered the question, "Why do you hunt?" They were instructed not to use a specific hunt or hunting season, but instead to respond in reference to their total hunting experience. Eighty percent responded with statements that fell into one of three categories: 1) development and testing of hunting skills; 2) nature appreciation and being outdoors; 3) escape and solitude. When asked, immediately after the close of a season, "What was the most satisfying aspect of the last season?" the largest percentage cited bagging of game. In a related study we asked over 400 deer firearm hunters attending pre-season hunting clinics to rate their anticipation concerning the coming season. In order, the five receiving the highest ratings were: 1) anticipation of a clean kill, 2) preparing equipment; 3) scouting; 4) return to particular locales or favorite hunting areas, and 5) practicing shooting skills.

When we analyzed the data in reference to hunter satisfaction, we concluded that motivation was highly dependant upon the time of year. Individual motivation resulted from goals that were identified and then individually operationalized by setting expectations. Once expectations were internalized, a plan for fulfillment was developed and an evaluation system designed to place value on the experiences, resulting in a satisfaction level. What hunters told us about their satisfactions caused us to become aware that goals, expectations, and motivations changed as the season changed. Prior to the actual hunt, the hunter's motivation was preparation, during the hunt it was harvest, and after the hunt it was reflection. "Why do you hunt?" is a question that encompasses a year round experience.

We became intensely interested in the issues that surround the topic of hunter motivation. When we studied data collected from rated satisfaction scales and responses to open-ended questions, the data appeared to be more symptomatic of motivation than the direct factors that contributed to one choosing to hunt. We compared it to a visit to a doctor's office. When the doctor asked what was wrong with a patient, the patient begins the process by explaining a series of symptoms. As the doctor listened to the various explanations, he/she began to interpret them and determine the real cause of the ailment.

We worked from the assumption that satisfaction would be best investigated by asking hunters to relate what was most satisfying about individual hunts.

When we studied the, "Why do you hunt?" data from both the whitetail and waterfowl hunters, most reported multiple satisfactions. The following list was compiled from the data; nature appreciation, companionship of fellow hunters, bagging game, escape and solitude, putting into practice hunting skills, perfecting ability to shoot accurately, pre-season scouting, reading hunting articles, watching videos, participating in food preparation, experiencing the rituals of the hunt, visiting with friends, preparing equipment for the upcoming hunt, exercise, provision of meat, opportunity to return to a cabin or land, sighting the game, and to be one against the elements of weather, were all indicators of satisfaction. A combination of the above list of satisfactions became each hunter's personal guide for evolution of his/her level of satisfaction.

We met with small focus groups to further explore the issues of hunter motivation, hoping to gain insight as to underlying causes.

Upon completion of the small group meetings, we believed there were four primary forces that motivated hunters to hunt. First, everyone desired time with oneself. Secondly everyone desired time with others. Thirdly, everyone desired to connect with the land. And fourthly, everyone desired to be part of harvesting.

When we take time to reflect and identify times in our own lives when it seemed like things were going well for us; we find that we had time for ourselves, we were participating in activities that were self-chosen and self-fulfilling, we had significant relationships with people who were important to us, and we were sensing the feelings that come with accomplishing goals.

Time For Self

As we listened to hunters grapple with the question of what motivates them to continue hunting, they consistently talked about their sense of well being when they were in the woods or marsh. Oftentimes, they mentioned the peace they felt in the quiet of the night before daylight or as the sun set and the woods filled with darkness; the fact that they were able to think so clearly and that problems seemed to have answers; what it meant to just relax and know they were just part of the world around them with no need to impress anyone or produce. They were talking about being at peace with one's self. Everyone needs their quiet place where they can go to be alone. Experienced hunters find that place while they hunt. I believe this was one of the basic factors that motivates a hunter to keep hunting.

In our initial interpretation of the data, we considered escape to mean that the hunter wanted to leave his/her world of work and responsibilities and retreat to the hunting area as a "getaway" from daily pressure. When we focused on the issues of motivation, we asked them to explain what escape meant. They explained a phenomenon of escaping to, not away from something. They hunted to have time to themselves, time to think, to reflect, to relate to friends, to relive memories, and to participate in their chosen venture. They hunted to have a place and a time to be themselves, the place where they had control of their time and choices.

Relationships

During small group discussions, hunters talked about how hunting impacted relationships. Father and son, brothers, cousins, the coming together of the family. The anticipation and preparation for the hunt that included their family. The meeting of fellow hunters in the hours before daylight, the anticipation of meeting again during the day or after the day's hunt ended. Stories of success and of the ones that did or didn't get away, jokes that were played on each other, funny stories of each other's experiences, pre-season and post-season meetings over coffee, sometimes a night out on the town, all centered around knowing, depending upon, and enjoying each other. Hunters hunt so they can experience relationships.

Hunting is primarily a male endeavor that legitimizes male relationships. Men have the need to have friends where they can develop close personal relationships, the same as women do, but in our society it is more difficult for men. Men are taught to be highly competitive, to hide emotions and feelings, to be physically and emotionally aggressive, and to be self-sufficient and independent which can rob them of the opportunity to meet the basic need to relate. Hunting breaks down these barriers. The hunt, which in ninety-eight percent of the cases is a partnership or group endeavor, allows the hunter to function in a group that has the common goal of harvesting game. The group becomes more successful as each member contributes to the group goal of the harvest, each member then gains in importance, the opportunity to honor and appreciate each other becomes legitimate, and deep appreciation and meaningful relationships form, which legitimizes the bonding.

Hunting provides the hunter with a place to retreat to be alone and to find peace with self. It also provides the opportunity for significant relationships through partner and group hunting. No other male competitive team activity allows for both needs to be met as all others are built upon high level, total involved energy being placed in the competition of the action. Peace for one's self does not exist. Hunting is unique. It is an activity that provides a place for self-fulfillment and relating.

The Land

All people have a basic need to connect with the land. All living things rely on the land for their survival, and each of us has a part in this survival plan. People will not be separated from the land. They will always find a way to experience it.

To realize that everyone has the need to be part of the land only requires that we watch children play. If there is dirt available, they will find it, dig in it, hold it, pile it, throw it, push it, and get it all over themselves. This basic need continues. Farmers and ranchers make their living from working the land. City populations move to suburbs where they have large lawns and gardens and land under their feet. People that stay in the city have smaller lawns and gardens. Those that live in apartments or homes with no land available have their plants in the house and go to parks and gardens of the city.

People plan vacations to connect with the land. They rent cabins on lakes or go to wilderness areas to camp, hike the trails in the forest, bird watch, study wildlife, flowers and plants, go to the beach and lay in the sun and the sand. Hunters hunt to experience the land.

Hunters study and learn the land and develop a keen appreciation of it. Of those interviewed, many related how strong their need was to return to hunting areas. Many talked about how they would return during the off-season and walk the land or how they had purchased land for hunting. If there was a hunting shack or cabin on the land, that added to the connection.

During our research hunters were asked why they chose the particular area they hunted. The number one factor was to return to a familiar area. The whitetail stand and the duck blind held high status as they were part of the constants that caused memories to flow and anticipation for the next season to emerge. They would explain, in great detail, the approach of a whitetail. The explanation took on descriptions of specific trees or shrubs that the deer would get behind or come around, of the continual stopping and looking around, the humps of land that it came over and finally, the position for the shot. Duck hunters talked about the relationship of the water to the marsh grass and the low shrubs, wind direction, circling birds as they worked their way in, all in great detail. Hunters knew the land, identified with it, felt an allegiance to it, and wanted to return. We were convinced that one of the most powerful forces that motivate hunters to hunt was their need to connect with the land.

They expressed an informed understanding of how nature depends upon cycles of life, and that as hunters they needed to respect the balances. They talked about the size of the whitetail herd in reference to the availability of food supply and the possibility of winterkill due to a severe winter. Water-fowlers related the need for nesting habitat for a healthy duck population and the need for harvest limits to assure that there would be future populations. What they said was that the land is capable of producing only a given amount, and by forming a partnership with the land, through good conservation practices and reasonable harvests, we can continue to have good hunting.

Hunters have an outstanding record of assisting in habitat improvement, wildlife restoration projects, and national, state, and local conservation projects both through financial support and direct labor. Hunters, more than any other recreational group, know, respect, and invest in the land. They return, year after year, to appreciate and harvest. To be connected to land was one of the primary reasons why they hunted.

Harvest

Everyone has a need to be part of a harvest. Watch people pick flowers from the seeds they planted, bring in the vegetables from the garden, walk on the lawn they planted, show you the surroundings of their yard when they have planted the trees, shrubs, and flower gardens; be with the farmers when their livestock goes to sale, when they pick the corn, combine the wheat, oats, and rye, and you know what it means to have a sense of accomplishment and pride.

Be with the hunter that comes out of the marsh with a limit of ducks or drags a whitetail to the truck, and you know what it means to have accomplished and to be proud. Harvest is when it all comes together - the planning, the investment, the risks and then the gathering in of the rewards. It is a basic need for everyone and hunters hunt to experience it.

My grandson, Zack, when thirteen years old and on his first whitetail hunt, shot a mature doe on the second morning of the season. He was about a hundred yards from me and there was heavy cover between us; it was planned that he was to come and get me if he got one. I heard the shot, waited, then saw him coming. The accomplishment, the pride, and sense of independence that was in his walk and on his face will forever be mine; he had experienced harvest.

I grew up in a potato growing area where the majority of the people made their living by working on the farms. Potato growing dominated the talk of everyone. It started with talk of waiting for the spring break-up so planting could begin, to the quality of the seed for planting, to the fear of insect damage during plant growth, as well as the concern of too little or too much rain. When the fall digging started, could it be finished before the first frost? The harvest involved everyone, the potatoes were picked by hand, the women left their homes to work in the fields, anyone who owned a truck was hired to haul the sacks to the warehouses for storage.

Work was focused and long hours were put in. Everyone was working together yet each individual was doing their own work and feeling the success of financial and personal rewards that comes from hard work. There was a feeling of consistent celebration.

The harvest is produced around a cycle from beginning to end. The cycle starts with birth and continues with the lifespan, the harvest, and then the replacement of the conditions that will lead to new birth. What draws all people to want to work the land and to be a part of the harvest is the need to be part of the cycle. Hunters hunt to be part of the cycle.

Each year I watch with curiosity the great shopping season that begins on Thanksgiving and ends at Christmas. It has all the characteristics of a harvest manipulated by commercial America. People who sell and people who buy have planned their strategies and they are put it into full-scale operation. It draws together families and small groups of friends for the single purpose of buying for others. It has its moments of success and moments of disappointment. It takes hard work and long hours. It requires an attitude of persistence. It produces an atmosphere of celebration as it nears its end, and it ends with a sense of personal satisfaction. Commercial America has created its own version of a cycle of harvest.

Hunting is harvesting. As we listened to hunters explain why they hunted, the element of harvest was one of the primary forces they explained. They talked about specific hunts and often related experiences of taking game. The hunt itself was explained from the preparation, the knowledge, the time in the field, the energy it consumed, the obstacles that had to be overcome, and then finally the taking of the bird or whitetail, which resulted in the final reward, feeling of accomplishment, and the celebration.

The four basic motivators, time for self, relating to others, connection to the land, and to experience harvest, are intrinsic aspects of the human condition. Hunters have found a way to positively express each of them. The individual hunter motivation and satisfactions from a hunt stems from connecting the basic four.

Compare the following results with your satisfaction scale responses. If you haven't completed the scale, do so before scrutinizing the following information.

Checklist From Results of 3,500 Hunters Rating of Satisfaction Scale

1. Development and utilization of hunting skills
2. Nature appreciation
3. Companionship
4. Escape and solitude
5. Use of specialized equipment
6. Development of outdoor skills (other than hunting)
7. Exercise
8. Testing of outdoor skills (other than hunting)
9. Competition
10. Harvesting game as a food source

1 = most satisfying
10 = least satisfying

CHAPTER 6
THE HUNTING PARTY

A hunting party is a group of hunters who hunt together without formal agreements. It differs from a hunting club which requires club designated and defined members, membership requirements, membership dues, a charter or constitution and elected officers. In this chapter the words hunting party and hunting group are synomonous and do not refer to a hunting club.

Hunting is primarily a group activity and the group could be uniquely important in controlling and influencing individual hunter behavior. As psychologists and researchers, we wanted to discover what, if any, influences the group might have on hunter behavior. What were traditions and practices of group hunting and what extent did the hunting group play in developing and facilitating safe, ethical hunters? To find out, we designed questions to help hunters reflect on the way they hunted. We looked at how they became hunters, what they anticipated from the hunt, and how their association within a hunting party affected all these factors.

We hypothesized that individual hunters would display high ethical standards when the group set such standards. When the hunting group defined standards and each member took responsibility to abide by and monitor each other and self, high hunting standards would be achieved.

Groups function by a basic principal of balance between productivity and cohesiveness. In the hunting group, productivity is exemplified as harvesting game, while cohesiveness is created by working together and building relationships. We discovered that as the hunting party became more effective at harvesting game, individual goals were replaced by group goals. For example, individual hunters who became part of an effective hunting group replaced their individual goal of filling tags or limits by adopting a group goal of sharing tags or limits.

Our research documented seventy-seven percent of Wisconsin gun whitetail hunters hunt in a group of three to ten, another eight percent hunt in groups of eleven or more, thirteen percent with a partner, and two percent hunt alone. Gun hunting in a group for whitetails was the standard.

It is fact that an individual within a group will take more chances and engage in higher risk-taking activities than individuals alone. We have all been part of a group where we laughed at jokes that weren't funny, said things we wouldn't say if the group members had not been present, and, at times, done questionable legal and ethical acts to find acceptance. Peer pressure, caused by the need to be recognized and to be part of a group, can work for either the good or the bad.

We designed hunting group interviews to probe how peer pressure would affect hunting groups. We wanted to determine how groups formed, how leadership developed, if there were defined rules that governed the hunt, and if the group had a positive or negative affect on the rate of violations. We contacted members of twenty-two hunting groups that had hunted together for more than ten years and told them of our interest and asked if we could meet with them. They were receptive and welcomed the opportunity to talk about their experiences.

The formation of hunting groups or parties primarily came into existence through one of three ways; family ties, land or home ownership, or friends that got together, often during their late teens or early twenties and stayed together. The friendship group often evolved into the development of a hunting shack or lodge, or they hunted out of a summer home that doubled as a hunting cabin during the hunting season.

The remainder of this chapter will list our conclusions as they related to each of the hunting groups. The conclusions enumerate how each of the groups formed, leadership style, group rules governing the hunt, and group position/response to violators.

Group Formation

The Family Group

Approximately sixty percent of long term hunting groups resulted from family ties. Eighty percent of the whitetail hunters we interviewed were introduced to hunting by a family member, and about fifty-five percent continued to hunt in the original family group. The family group developed traditions including specifically cooked foods on specific nights, eating out at the same restaurants on a particular night - typically a Friday night fish fry proceeding opening day, a big, hearty breakfast each morning, and sitting after the evening meal for talk, joking, and laughter. These strong family ties were talked about at length and with strong feelings. Many indicated the whitetail season, with the Thanksgiving holiday, was the only time the entire family assembled. Most indicated the only way to gain membership to the group was by family name or through marriage.

Land or Home Ownership Group

The second most common phenomenon that created a long term hunting group was when one of the members had ownership of land or a home in the hunting area, and friends or close acquaintances came for the hunt. These groups usually had some hunters who made up the main body of the group, having hunted together for years, with a more fluid membership that would hunt parts of the season. The core group members expressed enjoyment that only comes when hunting partners have a history of experience. There appeared to be somewhat open acceptance of new members who were invited by core members, and the number of hunters per day varied. The hunting group formed each morning, either in the woods or at the home of the leader. Some days there might be six or seven hunters, some days sixteen or seventeen.

Friendship group

The third group, the friendship group, more closely followed the formation of the family group. The hunters had usually hunted together for years, had a wealth of experience for recalling stories, often had invested money to build a hunting shack or stayed at one of the member's homes or cabin. They had a closed membership, primarily a father-son membership sequence or a very close friend of the senior members. They had a practice of traditional foods on certain nights, cooking sequences for members, often told the same favorite stories and expressed a deep sense of camaraderie. A whitetail was normally kept by the hunter who shot it, with a very informal procedure of distributing meat at the end of each season.

Leadership

The Family Group

Leadership did not appear to be of major significance in the family group and was often assumed by one of the senior members. The hunting methods had developed into a sequence that was repeated year after year. Each member had established an individual stand and if they decided to change, that was also a personal matter. They knew where each of the members had a stand, and were sensitive to not crowding or infringing upon others' territory. The first two days were usually spent standing, with each hunter responsible for harvesting his or her own deer. Often there were mid-day silent hunts to each other. Group hunting picked up as the season progressed and was usually accomplished through silent drives, with all members taking turns on the stands. There appeared to be adherence to unwritten rules established over time that governed the hunt during the latter part of the season. As the season progressed, the filling of tags became a group objective, and the objective of each member filling his/her own tag was replaced with group bag.

Land or Home Ownership Group

Leadership in the more fluid membership group that formed due to land ownership or a home in the hunting area was more pronounced. The predominate style of hunting was individual stands for early morning and evening hunts and midday drives. The owner of the land or home had the leadership role. He/she was responsible to choose the areas that would be driven, the placement of standers, organizing the pick up of the standers and drivers in the most efficient way, and had overall supervision of each hunt. It was understood that group bag was the standard and that each hunter would shoot whitetails for the party bag. Often the younger hunters were the drivers, and the more experienced hunters, with proven ability to shoot well, were the standers. The harvested whitetail were distributed to individual hunters by complicated formulas based upon the time the individual hunters hunted. Trophy racks went to the individual who shot the buck.

Friendship group

Leadership in the friendship group was normally provided by a senior member. The senior members, usually three or four, assumed a leadership role which was accepted by the remaining hunters. Leaders had responsibility to develop and enforce who was allowed membership, basic rules for living in the shack or lodge, if one existed, during the hunting season, and food planning. The hunting pattern had minimal need for leadership decision-making as the hunters had established stands which they continued to use year after year.

Individual hunting methods using stands and silent stalking were the standard throughout the season. A young hunter normally hunted with the father or the adult who had established the new member's right to hunt. This established member had the responsibility of finding the place to hunt and monitoring ethics of the new member.

Rules

We were interested in finding out if the groups had well defined rules that all members were made aware of and had agreed to abide by. Were there consequences if rules were broken? If rules were broken, who would enforce the consequences?

In all three of the groups it was difficult for members to identify where rules came from and the consensus was that they seemed to develop as the group continued to hunt together. Food traditions came about because members started to bring a particular food, often due to a self-perceived cooking specialty. Once the hunter introduced a particular food and it was well received by the group, it became a standard. They related that other rules, or what they rather called guidelines, came about the same way.

They stated that the process of arriving at the family home or the shack started the process of ritual, with members often stopping at the same restaurants and filling stations on their route to their destination. Year after year, different individual members often arrived within the same hour of the previous year, and each member's status was recognized as they arrived. Rules that governed the chores of dishwashing, housekeeping, and cleaning were again understood by all and the procedure for workers to do the jobs appeared to have developed over time and was adhered to by the members.

Bag Rules

Note: Group bag for whitetails in Wisconsin is legal.

Family Group

Bag for the family group usually followed the rule that each member fills their own tag during the first part of the season. It was understood that if a person had filled their tag and had the opportunity for a trophy buck, they could harvest the animal and it would be tagged by one of the other hunters. Group hunting, normally utilized in the latter part of the season, permitted any hunter who had the opportunity to shoot an agreed upon minimal rack size or sex to do so, and a member would tag it, as the group attempted to fill all tags. All groups who had young hunters attempted to have some antler-less tags that were reserved for them.

Land or Home Ownership Group

The hunting group that evolved from land or home ownership in the primary hunting area normally adhered to principles of group bag during the entire season. Group members often individually hunted early morning and evening stands, but deer harvested were considered part of the group bag. Throughout the day they followed a pattern of drives and abided by group bag guidelines. Individual hunters knew what the patterns and rules were, but they again had difficulty relating how they were originally defined and then agreed upon. The primary rules were the following:

If the opportunity arises, one hunter will shoot more than one deer.

Members who can hunt only on opening weekend will tag the first deer, having tags available for those who can hunt the entire season.

Young or inexperienced hunters get stands less likely to produce deer.

As the goal of filling tags for the entire group nears achievement, unsuccessful hunters get higher priority for stands that have a higher probability of producing a deer.

Hunters who have harvested a whitetail drive more as the season progresses.

Long Term Friendship Group

The long-term friendship group and/or hunting shack groups had no set guidelines for group bags. The standard was for each individual hunter to attempt to fill their own tag during the first part of the season and then the individual would let other members know if they wanted anyone else to fill their tag if the opportunity came about.

Safety Rules

Family Group

When asked about safety rules, the family group had the most defined rules and had often developed a system for monitoring them. The rules were directed toward the young hunter and pertained primarily to gun handling and hunting techniques. The rules would be instigated by any of the senior members. Example rules include:

Apprenticeship was required. Beginning hunters carried an empty gun or no gun at all for one entire season to demonstrate competence and earn the right to hunt.

Rifles with dangerous actions or semi-automatics were not

allowed to be used by beginning hunters. It was mentioned that beginning hunters would often use a breakdown shotgun.

Novices were placed near experienced hunters who monitor their actions.

Loading and unloading firearms among beginners and experienced hunters was supervised and constantly checked by any member of the party.

When hunting as partners, the experienced member would call out "freeze" and the beginner must stop and hold position. His/her behavior was then discussed in light of good safety practices and effective hunting methods.

<u>Land or Home Ownership Group</u>

There appeared to be minimal to no set guidelines for teaching or monitoring safety rules.

<u>Long Term Friendship group</u>

Safety rules pertaining to the young hunter were the responsibility of the adult who brought the individual into the party. There appeared to be no rules that were discussed and agreed upon by all members nor was there systematic monitoring for safe gun handling.

We were surprised that none of the groups had rules regarding shooting at deer during a hunt. When involved in a silent hunt through to each other or in organized drives, they had not set rules regarding the direct lines of fire which could have avoided the possibility of members being shot.

Alcohol

Of the twenty-two groups we interviewed, eighty percent said they had rules regulating alcohol usage during the hunting day. The three most commonly mentioned were:

There was no alcohol before the hunting day begins.

There was no alcohol usage during the hunting day.

Members were not to be in places where alcohol was served during the hunting day.

Violations

When each of the groups were asked about rules regarding violations, they all stated that violations were not a problem. We asked if they had discussed violations, set rules, and discussed the consequences if a hunter violated. They again stated that violations were not a problem. We asked what would happen if a member did violate and were told that he would be "on his own". It appeared to us that the different groups did not encourage violations, but did not address the issue either, nor did little in the way of consequences if a member did indeed violate.

Problem Areas

We asked if there were ever disagreements or problems between members of the group, and all of the group members said there had been. The most common problem focused on new membership. The family and long term friendship groups said it was difficult to keep membership from increasing as a member would like to ask a close friend to hunt on occasion, but this would often lead to the individual wanting to become a regular.

The land or home ownership group, being more fluid by design, had members bring along a partner that would turn out to be a detriment to the hunt or the group. When he was not welcomed back, the original member would become upset.

We asked how this problem was resolved, and the most common solution was that one of the senior members would tell the original member of the group that the new member was not welcome. We asked how other problems like vying for leadership, not satisfied with hunting procedures or practices, unsafe conditions, and not willing to do one's part in camp procedures were dealt with. The groups said the dissatisfied, on their own, normally did not return the next year.

Groups who had not developed rules that were discussed with all hunting members and agreed upon with understood consequences said they saw a need to do so, and planned on implementing them in the future.

We asked the groups what they would do differently if they had the opportunity to reform their group with a new beginning. We got answers that ranged from nothing different to everything different. We have taken some of their ideas and believe they could be used by groups to maintain and reinforce ethical, safe hunting. We recommend this be printed and possibly posted for all to see. Individual copies could even be handed out.

Gun Safety

If the hunting party has a shack or cabin where they stay or a home where they meet before the hunt, gun handling rules are posted, and one member reminds everyone to read them before leaving camp.

There is an understanding that if a hunter is either unaware or becomes careless regarding safety procedures, any member who sees an infraction has the obligation to correct that hunter.

Young hunters are consistently reminded and monitored on gun handling procedures.

Shooting Guidelines

Continual awareness of one of the golden rules of safe hunting, "Never shoot without knowing what is behind the target!"

The first reaction to seeing any moving or standing deer is that it is a hunter, be sure it isn't before you shoot.

During drives strict shooting guidelines are understood and absolutely abided by:

Standers shoot only at deer that have moved beyond them, never in the direction of the drivers.

Drivers shoot, if at all, only when a deer that has come back through the drive is going directly away from the drive.

Do all that can be done to allow each hunter to harvest his/her own deer.

General Guidelines

1. Violations are unacceptable. If a violation occurs, it will be reported and the individual can no longer be a member of the group.

2. There will be no alcohol consumed during the hunting day.

3.   Each member of the group will respect each other and participate in the hunt in a way that demonstrates a safe, ethical hunter.

The hunting party develops into a team of close personal friends and the goal of individual harvest of game transfers into a group goal where each member becomes an integral part of the overall harvest. When the group sets high ethical and hunting standards, the hunt becomes safe, an excellent place to teach young hunters safe gun handling and hunting skills, and extremely rewarding as individual hunters take pride in each other's hunting skill and harvest.

CHAPTER 7

THE SAFE HUNT

The following quiz could be used when you are in camp or during lunch or whenever possible to have a bit of fun with your hunting partners, and at the same time, reflect upon factors that equate into a safe, ethical hunt. The quiz was written by Homer Moe.

Hunter Responsibility Quiz

Score yourself and your hunting partner as follows:

Always - 10 points, Sometimes - 5 points, Never - 0 points

	You	Your partner
1. Is the firearm on safety until ready to shoot?	___	___
2. When unloading the firearm, are the ejected shells counted to assure the firearm is empty?	___	___
3. Are hunts planned in advance so the location of hunting partners are known at all times while hunting?	___	___
4. Have at least 20 rounds of ammunition been fired to become familiar with the hunting firearm?	___	___
5. Is florescent "hunter orange" clothing worn for deer and small game hunting?	___	___

6. Is permission to hunt always asked
for prior to hunting on private lands?   ___   ___

7. Are violations reported promptly to the local
   conservation warden?   ___   ___

8. Are firearms unloaded before crossing a
fence or other obstacles?   ___   ___

9. Are activities undertaken to support hunter
   education, hunter research, wildlife
   management, etc.?   ___   ___

                              Total Score: ___   ___

Scoring: 80 - 100 A hunter aware of responsibilities
              55 - 75   A hunter needing improvement
              0 - 50   Do not hunt with this partner

During one of the home interviews of a whitetail hunter, I interviewed a hunter whose son had been shot during a hunting incident. The accident occurred during a squirrel hunt and had not resulted in a fatality. The father wanted to talk about both his son and his son's friend who had fired the shot. During the discussion he said the accident actually had more of an effect on the shooter than on his son, and that the friend had quit hunting. What's more, the friend would no longer face the boy he had shot. This hunter was genuinely concerned for the young man.

Homer Moe, then administrator of the Hunter Education Program of the Wisconsin Department of Natural Resources, discussed with Bob and me his concern. "What were long term effects on the shooter in a hunting accident?" With Homer's expressed concern and the impact of the home interview, we decided to try to interview hunters who had accidentally shot someone while hunting. We decided not to do a structured interview, but instead, we would attempt to contact individuals who had been the shooter and ask permission to meet with them to talk about how the accident affected them.

Bob contacted the Wisconsin Department of Natural Resources and obtained the names of eight hunters. Five of them agreed to talk with me. I told them I was not in any way investigating the accident, not an employee of any state law enforcement department, that their identity would be kept confidential, and that I wasn't interested in details of the accident. I wanted to try to find if or how the accident had affected their daily lives.

During the time period I was talking with them, Bob worked on a study that attempted to determine the degree of accidental discharge of firearms and the occurrence of other hunting and non-hunting accidents involving firearms. I will first report the results of the accidental discharge study, then the shooter in a hunting accident.

Accidental Discharge and Occurrence of Hunting Accidents

Group interviews were conducted with 1,063 high school juniors and seniors from six states to determine the extent of accidental discharge of firearms and other field accidents. The interviewees were all graduates of hunter education programs.

In answer to the question, "Have you had an accident from an accidental discharge of a firearm?" twenty-two percent said yes. Twelve percent of the discharges resulted in injury, one forth of which was classified as major. Twenty-one percent caused property damage. When asked what they were doing during the time of the discharge, sixty-four percent said they were hunting, twenty percent were engaged in target practice, eight percent were cleaning their gun, and seven percent were coded as miscellaneous (horseplay, transporting the gun, dropped firearms, etc.)

These young hunters and shooters, an average of five years of firearm usage, were then asked to describe the accident. Of the twenty-two percent that stated they had an accident, twenty-one percent reported they had accidentally pulled the trigger, fourteen percent had forgotten the safety was off, fourteen percent had tripped or fell, seven percent described a clothing related factor, seven percent reported a firearm defect, and sixteen percent reported forms of horseplay.

An additional question asked if any of these young hunters had been with anyone else who had an accidental discharge accident. Twenty-four percent said yes. When asked what this companion was doing during the time of the accident, sixty-eight percent answered hunting, sixteen percent were target shooting, four percent were cleaning a firearm, and fifteen percent were miscellaneous.

Half of these companions were nineteen years of age or older. The largest percent, forty-four, of these individuals were said to be friends. Fathers were responsible for thirteen percent of the discharges, siblings for eleven percent, and other relatives and adults were responsible for thirty-two percent.

A third question pertained to the frequency of a hunting accident that did not involve a firearm. They were asked, "Did you or anyone with you ever have an accident, while hunting that didn't involve a firearm?" Twenty-seven percent answered yes. One third of the accidents involved a tree stand and another one-forth involved a fall from other than an elevated stand. Improper use of a knife was frequently reported. Nine percent of the accidents were not reported to authorities.

My personal reaction to the above statistics reaffirms the need for experienced hunters to set a model of the safe hunter for young hunters to emulate. I do not, in any way, see these statistics as a reflection on hunter education programs. The hunter education graduate has been introduced to safe firearm handling and safe hunting practices. It becomes the responsibility of experienced hunters to follow up on their initial training and to continually teach and monitor gun handling and safe hunting practices.

Shooters in a Hunting Accident

The average amount of time lapse between the accident and the five who were interviewed was five years. The interviewee was told in the initial contact that he did not need to talk about or describe the accident, and was told again at the beginning of the interview, yet each wanted to talk in detail about the accident.

One of the shootings occurred due to a misidentified target, one by a stander who shot at a deer that was in line with a driver, and three by drivers who hit another driver when shooting at deer that had cut back during a drive. None of the shootings resulted in a fatality, but the accident resulted in permanent limitations to each of the victims. In each of the accidents the individual shot was a member of the same hunting party as the shooter.

Each of the interviews started with skepticism on the part of the interviewee. They had to have assurances that I was not an employee or representative from the Department of Natural Resources, or an investigator, reinvestigating the accident. They needed assurance that what was discussed would not be used to identify them or as information to draw judgmental conclusions about them. We talked until they were assured that my only interest was to document what personal effect the accident had on them as they coped with the reality of the situation after the accident.

Once assurance was accepted, each of the five started to explain and, to a large degree, relive the accident. One of the incidents had occurred ten years prior to the interview and one had been within the year, yet all appeared to need to talk about the place, time, and facts of the accident.

I asked them if immediately after the accident they had the opportunity to talk about the accident with anyone. They all related they had answered a lot of questions from law enforcement investigators and tried to talk to family or close friends, but that it was impossible to sort out all their feelings and confusions. I asked them if it would have been helpful to have a professional trained counselor to talk with, and they said they did not know.

Each of them related that immediately following the accident there was a period of almost total confusion. They could not recall facts and had moments of disbelief that it happened. There were periods where there didn't seem to be any feelings or emotions, then a swell of emotion and guilt. Each talked about the sense of relief when the medical professionals assured them that the accident wasn't going to result in a fatality. I can only hypothesize that the feelings they expressed immediately after the accident would have been more intense had the accident been a fatality.

There was consensus by all five that after learning the victim would live, they entered a period of guilt, regret, and reliving the incident, trying to make sense of it. It appeared to me they attempted to justify their level of responsibility in the actual shooting. Was it really their fault? What could they have done to avoid it? They described how at times they were able to accept the reality of the shooting, the fact that it happened, and that they were the person who was primarily responsible, but then would relive the experience in an attempt to escape the reality.

Four of them had a significant time span between the accident and the interview, and each described a period of depression that followed the shooting. They explained that they didn't want to go out in public as they felt people would talk about them. One of the hunters had shot his father. He lived in a town of about seven thousand, and he said he couldn't go to the grocery store or anywhere in town as he felt that people were starring at him. He worked in a paper mill and I asked him about work. He said no one ever talked about the accident at work and that he hated to go to work, so he just went, did his job, and came home.

All four mentioned periods of headaches, stomach upset, and exhaustion. The person who had done the shooting within the year didn't describe the above stage, as he was still at the state of attempting to rationalize what had happened and what his level of responsibility was.

What helped them cope and begin to regain their self-confidence was when they could accept the fact that it was an accident. They said their support persons kept telling them it was an accident, and they knew all along that it was, but each one had to come to the point where they could individually accept it. I asked each one how they were able to reach that point, and it was difficult for them to articulate an explanation. They said it took time, a lot of thought, and they still had moments when they would rethink what happened.

I asked each if they still hunt. The one that had been in the accident within the year said he didn't know if he ever would. The other four had stopped. One of them said he had tried to return to the hunt, but whenever he heard a shot, it caused such anxiety that he simply could not deal with it.

I asked them what might have been done to avoid the accident. I found it interesting that they all said if each person hunted to shoot his own deer, the accident might have been avoided. Each of the shootings took place in a situation where there was party hunting and the goal was to group bag. Three of the accidents happened towards the end of the season when there was an attempt to fill doe permits. Two of the hunters said the added pressure of filling tags and environmental conditions were strong factors that contributed to the accident. One accident took place after a heavy snowfall that caused limited visibility. A deer ran back through the drive; the shooter, a driver, thought it was behind the driver next to him. With the snowfall causing hard going, the other driver had fallen behind and the bullet missed the deer hitting him.

Another of the hunters said they had to quit hunting by noon on the second Saturday of the season to attend a family wedding. There was a rushed feeling to fill the tags and he took a shot at a deer that was coming back through the drive. He hit one of the other drivers.

They talked about the need to set rules of firing when group hunting. None of the five hunted with a party that had set defined rules pertaining to shooting at deer during a drive. They continually emphasized the need to set rules and have them reviewed often.

Oscar and I are often joined by two or three other hunters during the last days of the whitetail-hunting season. We do silent hunts through to each other, attempting to slowly move deer in the direction of the stander. We know the land well and are now very careful to know exactly where the stander is and where the person who is still hunting will come out. There are no shots fired in the direction of either the stander or driver. We let the deer go if there is any possibility of shooting in the direction of each other. There are times when we line up, side by side, to push out a small dense area to standers. Drivers do not shoot and standers shoot only when the animal has passed beyond them. We didn't have these understandings before I interviewed the five. We do now.

The young hunter, who has gone through a hunter education program, has been taught the fundamentals of gun handling and to always know what was behind the target before shooting. The problem comes when they go from basic classroom and supervised line shooting to the actual field to hunt. If they are not modeled, both safe gun handling and knowing what was behind the target before shooting, the classroom learning can be quickly replaced by carelessness. It is the veteran hunter's responsibility to create safe hunters. Set rules, review these rules during the hunt, and monitor each other so the rules are followed.

After talking with the five men, I am convinced that when a shooting accident happens and there are life-long limitations or death to the hunter who was shot, there is a second victim who also places life-long limitations upon him/her self. The consequences from accidents never completely go away.

CHAPTER 8
INFLUENCES

Do you think the future of hunting is in jeopardy? Circle Yes or No. Jot down your ideas that support your choice.

Factors That Caused Us To Become Hunters

We were interested in documenting major influences that caused a young person to enter the hunting fraternity. Hunters typically enter the field at two points. Eighty percent enter at birth, having been born into hunting families who had a hunting tradition that had been developed over generations. The second point of entry was during the early twenties. The majority of these hunters had completed a post-high-school training program and found themselves in a work situation where their peers hunted. Through association with these peers, they were introduced to hunting. A second factor that introduced the post twenty group to hunting was marriage; they married someone who came from a hunting tradition and again, through association, a new hunter emerged.

Eighty percent of the hunters said they started to hunt because of family ties. For fifty-five percent, the major influence was the father. Brothers, sisters, and other relatives were credited by another twenty-five percent. Strong family ties were a key factor in developing interest and establishing tradition. Hunters talked about them at length and with strong feelings. Many indicated the deer season, with the Thanksgiving holiday, was the only time of the year the entire family assembled. One hunter reported that a brother flew all the way from Alaska to Minnesota to sustain the tradition. Despite our mobile society that tends to separate families, fifty-six percent of those interviewed were still hunting with at least one family member. Many said the only way to get into the group was through family name or marriage. A hunter's direct quote:

> "My uncle taught my cousins and me to hunt. He took each one of us when we turned twelve and had us hunt with him. He taught us all the same. Now we all hunt the same, think the same, and have fun during the hunting season the same. We hunt all season long. It's the best time of the year, and at the end of the season, we sit in the house and make plans for the next year. Then we wait all year for it to happen. My uncle is the most important person in my life."

Our study documented that the primary influences that caused a hunter to begin his/her hunting experience were their immediate family members, a relative, peers in the work place, or marrying into a hunting family.

During home interviews hunters were confronted with the question, "Why do you hunt?" and the usual response was one of hesitation, followed by carefully chosen words, as they pondered and attempted to match their words with their thinking. It appeared that some had previously attempted to answer the question on their own and, for many, it seemed to be the first time that they had actually thought through and attempted to explain their personal motivation.

During the discussion that focused on the, "Why do you hunt?" question, we often asked a follow-up question, "Why do you continue to hunt?" When we analyzed the data, responses focused on three points: the continual process of building a deeper sense of relationship with fellow hunters; the need to have time for self; and communing with nature.

We became interested in these three categories and followed up the findings by meeting with small groups of hunters to try to determine if there were common factors in their backgrounds that caused them to identify one of the categories. During the small focus groups, and hunters did indeed express a deep sense of commitment to the environment and an in-depth understanding of wildlife, which appeared to be two common threads that kept them hunting.

The small groups expressed ideas that coincided with the findings of Dr. Steve Kellert, who studied the attitudes of many types of humans towards animals. Kellert found that hunters fell into three categories: hunters who see animals in a utilitarian way - they hunt for the meat; the sport hunter who often demonstrates strong negativistic attitudes towards animals and who hunt to display their hunting skills and express prowess, competition, and master over the animal; and the naturalist who expresses great interest in wildlife, getting out in the woods, and indicating a basic affection and concern for animals and the natural environment. According to Kellert, the naturalistic hunter scored higher than any other hunter or non-hunter group on a knowledge quiz of animals.

The data we collected and analyzed, using the "Why do you hunt?" question produced the following results when hunters were placed into one of Kellert's three categories. Three percent of the duck and ten percent of the deer hunters were hunting for utilitarian reasons; seventy-seven percent of the duck and sixty percent of the deer hunters were sport hunters; and twenty percent of the duck and thirty percent of the deer hunters were naturalistic hunters.

The small groups used Kellert's categories, data from our studies, and their own personal backgrounds to analyze why they thought the majority of hunters were sport hunters. They came up with three rationales: 1) being that hunters primarily come from a rural or small town background, they had the advantage of being exposed to the environment and wildlife through direct involvement during their childhood; 2) each hunter recalled specific adults who had a profound influence on them by sharing or teaching them about the environment and/or wildlife; 3) they related that they were raised in a family that had minimal to moderate income and there wasn't money for major trips or vacations, but hunting season was a time when their family experienced a sense of departure from the routine of a work world and there was a feeling of excitement and anticipation present. This change of routine and sense of excitement had an affect on their attitudes and caused them to want to recreate it in their own adult world.

The only single identifiable factor amongst the hunters that caused them to become hunters was their infatuation with the gun or bow during their youth. They talked at great length about the first time they were able to hold a gun or bow, to admire it, and then their first shooting experience. As young boys, the sense of accomplishment and their feelings of entering the adult world through the carrying of a gun or bow were strong motivators that encouraged them to enter the hunter's world.

Each hunter that was independently interviewed was unique as each had their own story of why they hunted, what was important to them during the hunt, why they chose to become a hunter, and their deep commitment to the sport. Some hunted but one day out of a potential one hundred twenty days, some hunted almost all of the one hundred twenty days, most hunted somewhere in between, but the amount of time didn't affect their commitment and getting ready for the next one that dominated the talk.

Emerging Influences That Compete With The Desire to Become a Hunter

We have moved from a participatory to an observatory sports entertainment society. The professionalization of team sports with the publicity, salary, and advertisement frenzy has created a strong draw for the commitment of the young. They try the different sports out as young athletes, believe they could become a superstar, then develop an allegiance to the games with the final realization that very few become rich and famous. They then settle for becoming a fan and sit and watch. The stands and bleachers are full, and the television industry makes billions as the number of fans increases.

Wisconsin has a nine-day deer gun season that has shrunk

to one and a half day season for many of the 650,000 hunters who purchased a license. They hunt until noon on Sunday, and then retreat to a warm friendly environment with a television set that features the Packer game. Hunting season is over. If they have miles to drive, they depart their warm environment at the completion of the game and head home; if they live close by, they are already home.

Hunting is a demanding participatory sport that requires one to adjust to the demands of the weather, to be physically in shape, to be aware of and in tune with the environment, to be a student who reads and studies the literature to continually expand one's knowledge of the game that is being hunted, and to nurture perseverance to continue the pursuit. Success has come many times because we walked the extra mile, lasted out the wind and/or snowstorm, put on another layer of clothing, and stayed for those last few minutes of light, instead of heading for the truck. I believe the youth of today are looking for this kind of demanding adventure.

We have a monumental task when we attempt to introduce them to hunting, as it is difficult to compete with the hype that promotes false hopes of super hero status and wealth that comes from professional sports.

A second factor that has a significant bearing on the future of hunting is the urbanization of America. Rural America has and continues to shrink demographically and philosophically. The change from an agricultural dominated economy to an industry-driven economy to a future information-driven economy rearranges where people live and, ultimately, how they perceive the basics of life.

The hunting tradition originated in rural America out of necessity for food and provided a way of life that offered recognition and status for the proficient hunter. The people understood that to live, one had to be in touch with the land, know the land, and nurture the land, because when it would no longer give, life stopped. Hunting was part of the harvest from the land, and those that hunted were held in great respect. People who work the land, farmers, ranchers, and loggers, still understand that we are part of the land, not superior or inferior, just part of it, and that we must respect and nurture it if we are to be able to harvest.

Fewer and fewer individuals have the opportunity to understand and experience the land. The family farm is replaced with the corporate farm; the small logging operations are taken over by major operators and sophisticated, expensive machinery does the work. More and more of us loose touch with our true roots and the value of the hunt.

I was fortunate to have been born into a rural lifestyle that allowed me to develop my roots. My parents' self-sustaining lifestyle, the potato growers of the area, the small rural one-room school, the social gatherings of the community, card parties and dances at the town hall, the country store, the only store, the concern and outreach of neighbor to neighbor when need would arise, the common interest in our baseball team, and hunting all made the small village a good place in which to grow up.

I realized at a young age that all things in life have a cycle and that it begins at birth and ends at death. I saw the chicks hatch in the spring, grow during the summer, and be beheaded in the fall for food. I saw the calf be born, be fed for a few years, and then be butchered for our meat. Dad and grandpa's logging operation followed a cycle. In early December, immediately following the deer firearm season, they went into the frozen swamp to harvest spruce and tamarack. Spring break-up came in March with a rush to get the pulp skidded to a landing before the finalization of spring break-up. April and the first part of May was spent cutting jack pine. The poplars began to peel in May and June, and long days were spent cutting as many as possible. The trees were marked into one hundred inch pulp sticks, peeled and left to dry. July and August was back in the jack-pine stands, and then September and October were spent cutting and skidding the poplars, trying to have it out of the woods before the early snows.

November was butchering time, cutting the firewood for winter, and the whitetail hunt. I realized that trees grew to be cut, animals were raised for food, and that hunting was no different than harvesting trees or farm animals. The understanding of the internal balance of nature as it cycles is what is lost as America becomes more and more urbanized.

The village I grew up in no longer has a store or school. All the children go to a consolidated school district in a town of approximately eight thousand. Those who live outside of town are influenced and conditioned by the same influences as those who live in town. The people who live in rural, small towns, mid-size towns, or large cities are all subjected to a common perception of what constitutes the meaning of life, what is or isn't humorous, what events are significant, what we need to do to be a happy or contented person, and how they are, to think and act, to be recognized and become somebody. T h e urbanization of our society has little to do with where one lives, but instead it has created a homogeneity of thought and perceptions that are driven by mass media, up until now primarily through television and movies, and in the future equally so with the continuous advances of the home computer. We are subjected to the idea that major concerns that are of importance emanate from the city and pertain to people of wealth, political, or personal power and they are the important people who can, and do, solve problems. The media leads one to believe that if you are anyone of importance, you are from a metropolitan area, wealthy, have political position in a company organization or government, and are continually involved in questionable deals or relationships, but have the power and/or integrity to always solve the problems. The more we watch, the more we become disconnected from the land, the people who know and understand the land, the cycles of harvest, and basics of life.

I interviewed three men, each in their mid-twenties. Two of the men were hunters and one was not. All three came from a long held family hunting tradition and had been introduced to hunting by their fathers. I was most interested in the person who was not hunting, as the other two reported basically the same information as the majority of hunters who hunted due to family tradition. They talked about the strong family ties that emerged from hunting with their dad and brothers and how important the hunt was to the continuation of the family unity.

The one who did not hunt had quit when he was seventeen. He said during the five years that he had hunted, he enjoyed the days in the woods, but he often would think about the fact that he was missing the Saturday morning cartoons, and, most of all, he was missing time that he could have been doing competitive games and simulation on the computer. He said during the first few years he would be thinking, "I would really rather be home watching my favorite TV shows. Then, when I got into high school, I met and formed friendships with others that were into the computer world. It took on more importance than hunting."

Rural Americans and hunters are seldom featured in a positive way in either the television or movies because of what the media believes constitute marketable material.

When rural people and events are shown, they are stereotyped as uninformed, slow-thinking, simple-minded people who are out of touch with the real world. Hunters are projected as rural, dim-witted men who drive old trucks and have dogs that chase animals that are shot. People watch these shows and draw conclusions that hunters are uninformed, slow-thinking, simple-minded people who are out of touch with the real world.

I conducted a seminar for approximately seventy teachers in one of our large metropolitan areas along the east coast. The seminar pertained to classroom management techniques. It was a three-day training program and was being well received with high-level participation, enthusiasm, and continual positive feedback as to the practicality of the ideas. About half way through the third day, they realized I was an avid hunter. I could see and hear their disbelief that I could be advocating for children's rights, have a solid understanding of how and why children learn, and have a thorough and practical understanding of teaching techniques and still be a hunter.

We had broken down many of the barriers that keep people from feeling free to be honest when sharing ideas or from being able to question peers and then discuss the ideas that emerge, so they began to question me. After an hour or so of their questioning and their sharing about stereotypic perceptions of hunters, they commented that not one of them had ever personally known a hunter or had the opportunity to talk and discuss hunting with a hunter. I asked them where they got their perceptions of hunting and hunters, and they said from television and movies.

Will hunting be able to withstand the pressure of today's lifestyles by being able to compete for the time and, eventually, the allegiance of the young boys and girls to carry on the hunting tradition?

Status, based upon one's elevation of importance in both the peer group and community, has a strong influence on what young adolescents choose to do. Are there opportunities for the young hunter to build a positive peer group, or do sports, music, drama, the rebel, and the non-conformist monopolize their allegiance? As the community increases the importance on performance in high school athletics, drama, and music programs by highlighting them on television and in the newspaper, awards banquets, and school recognition programs, the more the allegiance to the particular program and therefore, the less the probability of in-depth involvement in hunting. Can we compete? The following chart indicates we are going to need a dedicated effort if we are able to change things around.

United States Hunting License Data

Year	# of Individual Hunters Nationwide
1977	16,197,015
1978	16,277,225
1979	16,551,886

1980	16,257,074
1981	16,638,584
1982	16,748,541
1983	16,372,904
1984	16,018,250
1985	15,879,572
1986	15,773,190
1987	15,812,528
1988	15,918,522
1989	15,858,063
1990	15,306,364
1991	15,718,865
1992	15,746,706
1993	15,627,763
1994	15,343,300
1995	15,232,338

1996   15,202,583

1997   14,906,862

Information submitted to U.S. Fish and Wildlife Service from state fish and wildlife agencies. These statistics show a decline of 1,291,189 hunters from 1977 to 1997.

The numbers reflect number of individual hunters, not the number of licenses sold as many hunters buys licenses in various states. After 1997, numbers were recorded on an every five-year schedule.

To investigate reasons for a hunter to stop hunting or for a young person choosing not to hunt was one of the objects of the study. We conducted interviews with twenty-seven active hunters who had adult sons and daughters that either initially or during their teen years had made the choice not to become hunters. We met with each of the fathers individually and asked them to respond to the question, "What do you believe caused young people to choose not to become hunters when there was a hunting tradition in the family?" We told them they were selected for the interview due to the fact that their adult offspring didn't hunt. We wanted them to respond from both a personal and general frame of reference.

They all related that they believed the number one reason for youth choosing not to hunt was due to lack of the father becoming involved with and influencing the son/daughter to hunt.

We asked them the follow-up question, "Why do fathers not get involved and encourage their children to explore the hunting world?" Their responses are summarized in the following six statements:

1. The age of twelve was too late to introduce youth to hunting. Many had already developed interests in other activities and those interests overpower the wanting to become a hunter.

2. Due to job and family demands, men don't have the time to develop an interest and involvement with their children.

3. Twelve of the twenty-seven interviewed had turmoil in their marriages that caused a separation or divorce. They stated that a separation or divorce resulted in the man losing respect in the family and reduced the probability of having major influences on the child during the formative years of early teens.

4. Some viewed hunting as an individual expression of who they were, and they were not overly motivated in having their own sons or daughters becoming hunters.

5. Their own interest in hunting was condensed into such a short period of time, due to seasons and demands of work, that there wasn't time to teach their children.

6. If the children were raised in a family where the mother was either not involved or negative towards hunting, it significantly increased the probability of the children not choosing to become hunters.

Is the future of hunting in jeopardy? I believe it is, if we as fathers and/or adult hunters are not willing to become involved with youth that express an interest in hunting.

We are competing in a diverse societal environment that appeals to our youth to become involved in extra curricular events at school, and projects negative imaging of hunters and hunting. Youth are continually exposed to urban values and lifestyles.

Therefore, without adult hunters becoming involved with youth hunting, hunting will diminish.

Research indicated that the following factors played a significant role in influencing young people to choose hunting as part of their recreational endeavors: a significant adult influence, most often a father, brother, or uncle who was willing and able to be involved with the youth and teach him/her hunting skills; the young hunter was able to find a peer group that hunted in which he/she could find acceptance; there was community support for promotion of hunting.

CHAPTER 9
The Research Model

On a Sunday morning, in 1972, after church, I was talking with Dr. George Gard, a biologist working for the United States Fish and Wildlife Service, stationed at the University of Wisconsin - Stevens Point. He knew I was a psychologist and hunter so he approached me with the thought that there was a need to develop a research base that pertained to the motivation, behavior, and ethics of hunters. He felt that the day was quickly approaching when hunting could be in serious jeopardy, and a research base was necessary to counteract the misconceptions that the general public held regarding hunters and hunting, as well as the need to prepare us for the anti-hunting organizations that were forming.

I had just joined the faculty at the University of Wisconsin - La Crosse campus, as a member of the Psychology Department and wondered if the department head, Dr. Bob Jackson, also an avid hunter, might be interested in the idea of a research project. I approached him and he immediately called Dr. Gard. Bob and I drove to Stevens Point, met with George, and on the 120-mile drive home to La Crosse, our project to study the motivation, behavior, and ethics of hunters was conceptualized.

As we designed the project, we made two major decisions. We would utilize a team approach involving hunters, professional members of the Hunter Education Program of the Department of Natural Resources, volunteer hunter education instructors and research statisticians for designing the research and interpreting the findings. The second decision was that the data we obtained would be produced through observational techniques, one-on-one interviews, and small group interviews. No data would be obtained by the use of self-report questionnaires.

Bob contacted the Wisconsin Department of Natural Resources, and Homer Moe, then administrator of the Hunter education Program, joined our team. During his leave of absence from the department to serve as NRA Hunter Education Director, his replacement, John Plenke, came on board. They were both invaluable resources to the project, as they involved the six Wisconsin Department of Law Enforcement Safety Specialists, who consistently contributed ideas for the project, had meaningful insights about hunters, the education of first time hunters, assisted with interpretation of data, and informed us of key individuals for inclusion of research ideas as well as funding sources at both the state and national levels.

The project began in 1972 and continued through 2001. Our first project was to obtain data on duck hunters. Duck hunting, due to low duck populations, was under pressure by non-hunter organizations as well as anti-hunter groups operating under false assumptions that hunting was the major contributor to the low numbers.

We designed an observational and follow-up interview study format. Outside funding and internal funding from the University was obtained. Bob and I were released from our full-time teaching responsibilities, and we recruited several retired conservation wardens. We began to hire and train university students to do in-field observations, which resulted in 650 hunters being observed, and their hunts recorded.

The students observed the hunters from spy blinds as they hunted and recorded hunter behavior on two-minute intervals. When the students observed that the hunt was ending, they left their observation positions to return to the landing prior to the hunters' return so they could do an in-field interview with the hunter. The hunters were not informed that they had been observed. The in-field interview focused on the hunters' interpretation of the immediate hunt by asking questions about their behavior and satisfaction of the just completed hunt. They were then asked if they would be willing to participate in a follow-up two-hour home interview.

The duck hunter project continued, and we introduced the whitetail deer hunter project. We interviewed 1,100 whitetail deer hunters immediately after their hunts, either at their vehicles or in the field. These interviews were followed by 258 one-on-one, two-hour home interviews, taken from a random sample of the in-field interviews.

As the two projects continued, we started a landowner study project with 106 landowners. The project was designed to document the landowners' perceptions of hunters. We petitioned for landowner volunteers through local newspaper ads, then contacted respondents by telephone and explained the research. We selected participants that represented a statewide Wisconsin sample. They were asked to keep a log of their observations during the nine-day firearm season and participate in a two hour one-on-one interview at the conclusion of the hunting season.

The fourth major project focused on bow hunting. We interviewed hunters in the field immediately following a hunt and then followed up with extensive in-home interviews to document their perceptions of their own behavior, ethics, and motivation as a hunter and to reflect in the behavior, ethics, and motivation of other hunters. We conducted 268 field interviews, completed 100 home interviews, and interviewed 22 bow-hunting clubs.

We continued to have outside funding sources, through 1985, which allowed Bob and me to have release time from our teaching responsibilities to work extensively on the research. The major funding was provided through the Fish and Wildlife Service, utilizing Pittman Robertson funds which is money generated by a tax on the sale of guns, ammunition, and archery equipment, and channeled through the Hunter Education Program of the Wisconsin Department of Natural Resources. Individual sportsmen, and local, state, and national affiliation organizations also contributed to the project.

The hard data gathered from 1977 through 1985 in-field observations, in-field interviews, and in-depth home interviews was used as the basis for interpretations and findings and for baseline data for future research. From 1985 through 2001, due to limited funding, Bob and I had to return to full-time teaching. The research then centered on specialized projects where smaller numbers of respondents were adequate to determine findings. We continued to utilize one-on-one interviews and small-group interviews to study: the habitual-professional violator; the shooter involved in a hunting accident; rate of accidental discharge and non-shooting accidents; women that were married to hunters, fathers of sons and daughters who, as adults, chose not to hunt; in-depth analysis of hunter satisfaction and motivation; reasons why hunters stop hunting; bow hunters who have only hunted over bait; and continued analysis on the stages of hunter development.

The observations, interviews, small group meetings, and

hunter responses to our professional published articles always focused around the same three anticipated outcomes: "Why do we hunt?" - the motivation; "How do we hunt? - the ethics; and, "How do we behave when we represent ourselves as hunters, both in and out of the field?"

One of our original objectives was to conduct a longitudinal study where we could follow young, beginning hunters over a significant time period to document how they developed as hunters. What influences caused them to change, both behaviorally and technically? Did their interest in hunting intensify or diminish? How did they influence the future of hunting? Due to financial and time constraints, we were not able to do this aspect of the research, but we do believe we have an accurate picture of how hunting affects the individual hunter and how the hunter affects hunting. The information for the book was drawn from a pool of over 5,000 hunters.

About the Author

Dr. Bob Norton, Professor Emeritus
University of Wisconsin
La Crosse campus

Dr. Norton joined the faculty as a member of the psychology department at UWL in 1972. He taught in the graduate program and was involved, with his colleague, the late Dr. Bob Jackson, in conducting the research program entitled, The Behavior, Motivation, and Ethics of the Sport Hunter. The U.S. Fish and Wildlife Department of the Wisconsin Department of Natural Resources sanctioned the project.

Dr. Norton is an avid outdoors person. He is addicted to musky fishing as well as hunting. His favorite upland bird is the grouse as well as spending much time hunting ducks in the backwaters of the Mississippi River bottoms. He lives to bow hunt whitetails and has rifle hunted them in Wisconsin for fifty-four of the last fifty-six years, missing two years while serving in the Army.

NOTES

NOTES

Essential Books for the American Hunter

The Hunter: Developmental Stages and Ethics
By Bob Norton, Ph.D.

"This research and its impact on hunters and hunter education instructors are phenomenal."
   Homer Moe, former administrator of the Wisconsin Hunter
   Education Program, Wisconsin Department of Resources

Beyond Fair Chase: The Ethic and Tradition of Hunting
By Jim Posewitz

"Jim Posewitz has laid out, clearly and decisively, what may be the deciding factor as to whether hunting will (or should) remain a part of American culture. As a hunter and a conservationist, I say—it's about time."
   Jack Ward Thomas, former chief, USDA Forest Service

Inherit the Hunt: A Journey into the Heart of American Hunting
By Jim Posewitz

"Hunters: Put that magazine aside, shut off the television, maybe even give up a few hours in the woods if that's what it takes—but make sure you read this book. It could be the most important thing you do if you care about the future of wildlife and hunting."
   Richard Nelson, author of *Heart and Blood*

Rifle in Hand: How Wild America Was Saved
By Jim Posewitz

"A splendid book. It is not merely enlightening and a joy to read, but I found it moving as well in places. And not too many books have done that to me."
   Dr. Valerious Geist, Professor Emeritus, The Universtity of
   Calgary

For more information about these books, including special discounts for hunter education programs and conservation groups, call Riverbend Publishing toll-free 1-866-787-2363.